150 Years of Racing in Saratoga

LITTLE-KNOWN STORIES & FACTS FROM AMERICA'S
MOST HISTORIC RACING CITY

ALLAN CARTER & MIKE KANE

Charleston · London

THE
History
PRESS

Published by The History Press
Charleston, SC 29403
www.historypress.net

First published 2013

Manufactured in the United States

ISBN 978.1.62619.102.0

Library of Congress CIP data applied for.

To our friend Richard L. Hamilton, a man of many interests and talents: voracious reader, teller of stories, expert on racing silks, insufferable fan of the Red Sox, mentor, comedian, historian, language maven, kind and caring person and lifelong fan of Thoroughbred racing.

Gone, but certainly not forgotten.

Contents

CONTENTS

Preface

While there were deadlines, there was no start date to this project. It began to happen during the nearly five years we spent together at the National Museum of Racing and Hall of Fame. During our many conversations, we talked about creating a book together some day.

The concept we agreed on was to write about subjects that interested us and might entertain readers. Hugh Bradley, Ed Hotaling, Mike Veitch and other authors have turned out fine histories of racing in Saratoga Springs, so there was no need for another. We decided to give the often-told Saratoga stories a pass and focus on little-known subjects that might have been overlooked or given scant coverage. That opened the door for chapters about Los Angeles and Checkmate, Saratoga owner Gottfried Walbaum, firsts at the track, some of the great matchups, the reasons that led to the track being closed for a total of six seasons and stats from the decades before the New York Racing Association (NYRA) bought the track.

Allan and I have a few things in common. We are natives of the nearby city of Glens Falls who had little to do with racing in our youth but embraced the sport as adults. We have a love of history and enjoy researching, writing and talking about the past. For Allan, the introduction was as a fan in the late 1960s; mine was as a journalist at the end of the '70s. We came to appreciate that we were raised, work and live close to America's greatest racetrack—so close, in fact, that Allan walks to the track most every day of the meeting.

We were introduced one morning in April 2005 by our mutual friend Richard Hamilton. Allan had succeeded the legendary Tom Gilcoyne, who had decided as he approached ninety that it was time to retire as the historian at the National Museum of Racing. Hamilton was sliding into retirement, too, and I was taking over his position as the communications officer.

Thanks in no small part to Allan's persistence, eight years later there is another Saratoga book to add to the library.

—MIKE KANE

Acknowledgements

T wo names are on the cover, but this book could not and would not have been written without the help of many other people.

At the top of our long list of people to thank is Chris Dragone, director of the National Museum of Racing and Hall of Fame, for his enthusiastic encouragement and for giving us carte blanche in our use of the museum's images. A special thanks goes to Arianna Galluzo, assistant curator at the museum, for the countless hours she spent providing us with the photos we requested and scanning the ones we selected. It was a lot of work, and she did it with a smile.

Others who assisted us in acquiring the images we wanted were Teri Blasko and Victoria Garlanda of the Saratoga Room of the Saratoga Springs Public Library; "Sam" Hildebrandt of Friends of Sanford Stud Farm; longtime California racing photographer Bill Mochon; NYRA photographers Adam and Bob Coglianese, whose family has been recording racing history for decades; Cathy Schenck and Amy Petit of the Keeneland Library; Jamie Parillo of the Saratoga History Museum; the National Museum of Racing's Brien Bouyea; and Minnie Bolster, who has witnessed and recorded many decades of life in Saratoga Springs.

Bill Cavanagh, Jim Sweet and Joe Peck put in countless hours as research volunteers in the library at the racing museum, and their dedication yielded the trove of statistics published for the first time in these pages. In Kentucky, Bill Mooney, Ed Bowen and Rhonda Norby promptly found the answers to some vexing research questions.

ACKNOWLEDGEMENTS

Jim Melia, Mike Veitch, Joe Cacciolfi and Bob Curran graciously offered time to proofread what we had written, keeping our "howlers" to a minimum.

The late Mike Burke was able to return to his hometown for his final years and became a close friend, inspiration and source of ideas and information. His research proved to be invaluable. We still regret his premature passing.

Thanks, of course, to Whitney Landis at The History Press, a native of Saratoga Springs, who made it possible for this book to be published, as well as to her colleagues for getting everything together.

Finally, we would like to thank our wives, Paula Carter and Kathy Kane, for their support and patience and, in Paula's case, for her IT assistance to her Luddite husband.

First Things First

The Thoroughbred racing era in Saratoga Springs began on Monday, August 3, 1863, with a pair of races on the trotting track on the north side of Union Avenue in what was later renamed Horse Haven. Eight races were contested over four days in that inaugural meet arranged by John Morrissey. Buoyed by the success of that experiment, Morrissey and his partners purchased acreage across the street and built a venue on the grounds of what is now Saratoga Race Course. There have been plenty of "firsts" since that 1863 launch. Here are several of note.

FEMALE JOCKEYS

Robyn Smith was the pioneer female rider at Saratoga Race Course, and she accomplished the double of the first ride and first victory.

Smith, an attractive woman with a somewhat mysterious past, made history on Monday, July 29, 1970, when she rode Embecias in the second race of the opening day card. Embecias, a three-year-old filly trained by Frank Wright, finished ninth in the ten-horse field of maiden claimers. The *Saratogian* gave it top-of-the-page coverage in the sports section.[1]

"I've always wanted to go to Saratoga," Smith said. "Riding here is a real privilege."

Jockey Robyn Smith was the first woman to ride at Saratoga and to win a race at the track. *Courtesy of NYRA/Bob Coglianese.*

Wright noted, "Miss Smith definitely has some real ability. If any girl is going to make it as a result of application and effort, I think she might very well be the one."

Women broke through and started riding in pari-mutuel races in 1969, but no one reached the starting gate at Saratoga that summer. Two female riders tried, though. According to an Associated Press report in the *Schenectady Gazette*, Patty McDonald, the wife of steeplechase jockey Bob McDonald, was named on a horse that was scratched early in the meet. The New York Racing Commission prevented Ann Walsh from riding Safe Corner because her husband owned the horse and jockeys were not allowed to have a financial interest in their mounts.

Smith broke a track record when she recorded the first victory by a female jockey at Saratoga in the fourth race on Saturday, August 14, 1971. Riding Hobeau Farm's Beaukins for trainer H. Allen Jerkens, Smith set a seven-furlong record of 1:21 4/5. Beaukins had to run fast in the $15,000 allowance race on the Alabama program to beat a very strong field that included Queen's Plate winner and Canadian champion Kennedy Road, the accomplished stakes filly Process Shot and 1970 Whitney winner Judgable. Under Smith, Beaukins shaved two-fifths of a second off the record and paid $16.20.[2]

On August 20, Smith won again on the Jerkens-trained Roman Consort. She was named to ride Ellen's Voyage in the 1971 Travers, but the horse was scratched.

When she started riding in 1969, Smith was portrayed as a native of Hawaii who was an English major at Stanford and a Hollywood starlet. Much of that turned out not to be true, but she apparently was taking acting lessons before she turned to racing in California. Smith rode for about a decade and in June 1980 married entertainer Fred Astaire, who at eighty-one was forty-six years her senior. He died in 1987.

Trailblazing rider Kathy Kusner was the first woman to ride a steeplechase horse in a race at Saratoga on August 10, 1971, when she finished fifth on Pilgrim's Progress.

Hall of Fame jockey Julie Krone was the first female jockey with a Travers mount when she rode Belmont Stakes winner Colonial Affair to a fourth-place finish in 1993. Two other women have ridden in the Travers: Emma-Jayne Wilson, sixth on Moonshine Mullin in 2011, and Rosie Napravnik, tenth on Five Sixteen in 2012.

PHOTO-FINISH CAMERAS

The electric-eye cameras were introduced in the New York tracks in April 1936 and were in use at Saratoga that summer.

SUNDAY RACING

The New York Racing Association experimented with Sunday racing in 1975, and the first card was held at Saratoga on August 3.[3] The nine-race program drew a crowd of 13,841. Bold Forbes won the feature, the Saratoga Special. That historic Sunday program drew the smallest attendance of the week. Business picked up on the other two scheduled Sundays: 21,085 on August 10 and 23,408 on August 17.

NYRA backed away from Sunday racing at Saratoga until 1979, when it moved to the Wednesday through Monday schedule with a dark day on Tuesday that remains in effect. The first Sunday program that summer drew a crowd of 19,369, which turned out to be the smallest of the four Sundays.

PARI-MUTUEL WAGERING

In 1939, the people had approved an amendment to the state constitution allowing pari-mutuel betting in New York. Saratoga entered the modern era of racetrack gambling with the opening of the 1940 season on Monday, July 29. New York passed legislation sponsored by Senator John J. Dunnigan requiring use of the pari-mutuel system. In pari-mutuel wagering, gamblers compete among themselves for the money in the mutuels pool, and odds change as money is bet on each of the horses in the race.

The Saratoga Association spent a reported $200,000 preparing the plant for the tote system. A total of 307 mutuel windows were installed at eight locations around the track. The *Saratogian* reported that 169 windows would be used for selling tickets, 128 for cashing and 10 for change and information. The entire operation would be staffed by a crew of 450 people.

There were some problems on the first day of the season: the program ran late, and the first post for the remaining days was moved ahead. The season opened with a steeplechase, and the first pari-mutuel winner at the Spa was Big Rebel, who paid ninety-eight dollars. Since the move to pari-mutuel was big news leading up to the start of the season, the payoff made headlines.

Wagering with bookmakers was a storied and sometimes controversial part of the Saratoga racing experience. The arrival of the Cavanaugh

The Saratoga Association built 307 windows for the debut of pari-mutuel wagering in 1940. *Courtesy of the Saratoga Room, Saratoga Springs Public Library.*

Special, the train carrying bookmakers and gamblers from New York City to Saratoga Springs, was widely reported in newspapers as the opening act of the season. As a result, the change to pari-mutuel at Saratoga was not embraced warmly.

Track Announcer

Fred Caposella was a well-known track announcer in New York for nearly forty years, but the first announcer at Saratoga Race Course was Bryan Field, the longtime turf writer for the *New York Times*. Field, who was a broadcaster and a track official during his long career, was the first announcer at the track in 1940.

In a preseason article, the *Saratogian* wrote about the improvements made under the direction of track president George Bull: "Three new radio booths have been built by Mr. Bull and every big race will be broadcast by Bryan

Field for the Mutuel network, Clem McCarthy for NBC and Ted Husing on the Columbia chain. In addition, a most up-to-date public address (loudspeakers) system has been installed and Bryan Field will describe each race over it as they are being run."

Caposella was a stalwart at Saratoga until his retirement in 1971, when he was succeeded by Dave Johnson. Early in 1977, Johnson and NYRA announced that they could not agree on a new contract, and Johnson was replaced by Chic Anderson. Two years later, in March 1979, Anderson died of a heart attack at the age of forty-seven. Marshall Cassidy took over and called races through the end of the 1990 Saratoga meeting. Since then, Tom Durkin has been the main NYRA announcer.

TURF COURSE

The group headed by William C. Whitney that purchased the track in December 1900 began a major rebuilding project following the 1901 season. One of the changes was the addition of a one-mile turf course inside the new dirt course. The turf course was seeded in 1902, and the first race held over it was the 1903 Alabama Stakes on August 4.

Thirteen races were run on the turf in 1903 and six the following summer. However, flat racing on the grass was discontinued, and the space was used for steeplechase competition. A new turf course was installed in 1961. In 1993, it was named in honor of the prominent owner and philanthropist Paul Mellon.

NYRA started using the seven-furlong hurdles turf course for flat racing in 1978.

ELECTRIC STARTING GATE

The new portable gate, designed to control horses and provide a fair start for all, debuted on the opening day of the 1940 season. Other starting devices had been used from the late 1920s, including permanent stalls in the seven-furlong and mile chutes.

FEMALE TRAINERS

Mary Hirsch was the first female trainer to win a race at Saratoga when No Sir captured the Diana on August 27, 1936. In those days, the Diana was a race for horses owned by women. She is listed on the chart of the race as the owner and trainer of No Sir, who started in the 1937 Kentucky Derby.

It is quite possible that she trained other winners before the Diana that were listed in the names of her Hall of Fame family members: her father, Max, and her brother, W.J. "Buddy." Mary Hirsch received licenses from state racing boards in 1934 and was finally licensed by The Jockey Club in 1935. She was the first and still only female trainer to win the Travers with Thanksgiving in 1938.

Linda Rice was the first woman to win a training title at Saratoga, or any other major track, in 2009,

Linda Rice was the first woman to win a training title, with twenty victories in 2009. *Photo by Mike Kane.*

when she edged Todd Pletcher by one victory. Pletcher has won multiple Saratoga titles among his many accomplishments and is a shoo-in for election to the Hall of Fame when he becomes eligible. Like Pletcher, Rice grew up in a racing family. She started training in 1987, developed a solid reputation and found success.

Winning the meet title at Saratoga was an unexpected bonus. Focusing on grass racing, often in turf sprints, she won with 20 of her 75 starters. Eighteen of the wins came on turf. Pletcher sent out 134 starters.

"This is as good as I've ever felt," Rice said. "It's an absolute thrill. This took a lot of years and a lot of hard work. It took a long time and a lot effort to get here. This is the type of thing you just don't think will ever happen. To walk into the winner's circle and get awarded with the leading trainer title and be the first woman to do that at a major race meet just makes it that much more special."

EXOTIC WAGERS

While multi-horse and multi-race bets, like exactas and Pick 3s, are now available on every race on the program, the wagering menu was limited to straight win/place/show action during the first eight decades of racing in Saratoga Springs. The first daily double in Saratoga history was offered on July 28, 1941. Speculate won the first race, and Porter's Girl won the second. A mere twenty-nine years later, exactas were added to the menu in 1970. Trifectas debuted on July 29, 1974. Quinellas became part of the betting options on August 1, 1979.

JOCKEYS

James McLaughlin was the first rider to win four races in one day when he swept the card on August 13, 1883.

Angel Cordero Jr., the dominant rider at the track in the 1970s and 1980s, reached the five-win milestone on July 31, 1968. Since then, four other riders—Ron Turcotte, Julie Krone, Mike Smith and John Velazquez—have had five winners on a single program. Velazquez was the first rider with a six-win day on September 3, 2001. In 2012, Ramon Dominguez had two six-victory days.

Leading rider Ramon Dominguez had the second of his six-win days in 2012 on September 3. *Photo by Mike Kane.*

Whichone

The "Other" Horse in the 1930 Travers

Most serious horse fans, and even casual fans who make an annual trek upstate to Saratoga, know that Jim Dandy was the 100-1 shot who upset recent Triple Crown winner Gallant Fox in the 1930 Travers. It's a safe bet that few could name the other two horses in the field that day.

One of them, Sun Falcon, is merely a historic footnote who was unable to break his maiden until the seventh race of his three-year-old season. On the other hand, Whichone was considered one of the best horses of his generation until he suffered a career-ending bowed tendon during the running of that legendary Travers.

A 1927 foal by the imported French stallion Chicle out of the Broomstick mare Flying Witch, Whichone was a homebred from the powerful Harry Payne Whitney stable and was trained by James Rowe Jr. After losing the first race of his career and winning the second, both at Aqueduct and both as the favorite, he was brought to Saratoga.

Whichone won his first start in the summer meet, a two-year-old allowance race, once again as the favorite, and he made his stakes debut on August 16 in the Saratoga Special. Sent off as the 1-2 favorite against eight other horses, he won by five lengths despite a slow start. The Saratoga Special was a winner-take-all race, earning $16,500 and a gold cup for Whitney.

The *New York Times* turf writer Bryan Field was suitably impressed: "Few horses have outclassed their fields the way Harry Payne Whitney's Whichone did this afternoon in winning the Saratoga Special…That he could run so fast as to overcome this handicap [a bad start] and add a six-

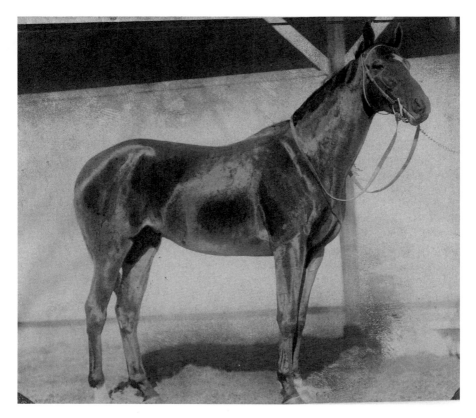

The 1929 champion two-year-old Whichone was third behind Upset and Gallant Fox in what turned out to be his final race. *Courtesy of the Keeneland Library.*

length advantage in the two furlongs of the stretch run remaining is the best measure of Whichone's speed and caliber. Moreover, he was going easily at the wire, stepping high and handsome."[4]

Whichone's next race was Saratoga's prestigious Hopeful Stakes, pitting him against Boojum, who had won his first two starts. Boojum was another Whitney homebred by John P. Grier out of a Chicle mare, Elf. Whichone and Boojum comprised an imposing 1-4 entry against ten other opponents. Although neither horse got off well, the entry eventually assumed the lead coming into the home stretch, with Boojum winning by a neck over his stablemate. Five lengths back in third was Caruso, and finishing last was a 40-1 shot named Jim Dandy.

Boojum set a new American record of 1:17 for the 6½-furlong distance. Although Boojum was getting eight pounds from Whichone, he was nevertheless the new leader of the two-year-old male division. That leadership position was short-lived, though. The two horses moved downstate to Belmont Park after the Hopeful, with the Champagne scheduled for September 7 and the rich Futurity a week later. Whichone swept both two-year-old events, with Boojum finishing third in the Champagne and fourth in the Futurity.

There was much interest in the Champagne because of the presence of the Whitney entry, which, not surprisingly, went off at 1-7. It is possible that if the two had not been an entry, Boojum might have snapped Whichone's streak of having been a favorite in every race he had run up to that point. In fact, in the custom of the period with entries, Whitney declared Boojum to be the winner.

Whichone came off the pace to win by a length over Gone Away on a muddy track, setting a new stakes record of 1:21. It might have been faster if Whichone's jockey, Pony McAtee, hadn't bided his time while Boojum was in the lead to ensure Whitney's declaration. Once it was evident that Boojum was faltering, McAtee alertly sent his mount to the front, and Whichone regained his leadership of the two-year-old male division. Ironically, Whichone's sire, and Boojum's maternal grandsire, Chicle, had won the 1915 Champagne.

The Futurity, the richest horse race in America, drew seventeen starters, and once again Whichone and Boojum were the favorites, this time at 2-7. Boojum, as usual, assumed the lead, but Whichone took over at the half and won easily with no urging from McAtee's whip. Hi-Jack was second, and in third was the thus far unheralded 20-1 Gallant Fox.

Whichone's victory in the Futurity added $105,730 to his final earnings total of $135,455, making him the richest two-year-old and second-richest horse, behind future Hall of Fame inductee Blue Larkspur, in the country. In another family note, Whichone's full sister, Mother Goose, the only other foal of Flying Witch to amount to anything on the track, won the 1925 Futurity. Both Whichone and Mother Goose were named champions of their respective divisions by Thoroughbred Heritage. Whichone was a clear-cut winner, while Mother Goose shared honors with her Whitney stablemate, Maud Muller.

Whichone began his sophomore season on May 28, 1930, with a win in an overnight stakes at Belmont, followed three days later by a walk in the park in the Withers as the 1-10 favorite. His first big test of the year awaited him on June 7 in the 1½-mile Belmont Stakes. Facing him would be the late-developing Gallant Fox, who had followed a mediocre 1929 season with wins in the 1930 Wood Memorial, Preakness and Kentucky Derby prior to the Belmont.

Despite that impressive record, Tom Shaw, the New York betting commissioner, increased Whichone's favoritism status from 7-5 to 4-5 following his win in the Withers. Gallant Fox was Shaw's second choice in the Belmont at 7-5. A rainstorm on the day of the race downgraded the status of the track from fast to good, and bettors made Whichone the 3-5 favorite, while Gallant Fox went off at 8-5. The "Fox of Belair" won the race with comparative ease by three lengths, while Whichone, whom the chart had stated "did not stride freely in the greasy going," made a late rush to finish second. Questionnaire was third and Swinfield a distant fourth.

Gallant Fox, the first horse to be credited with winning the Triple Crown— though eventually Sir Barton was recognized as the first to sweep the series— was the new leader of the three-year-old colt division. After his win in the Belmont, he won the Dwyer at Aqueduct and the Arlington Classic, giving him six wins, all stakes, in as many starts going into the Travers. Whichone resumed his winning ways at Saratoga by easily taking the Saranac Handicap, Whitney and Miller at odds of 1-2, 1-12 and 1-8, respectively.

Although the morning line stamped Gallant Fox as the slight favorite going into the Travers, the *New York Evening Post*'s correspondent still felt that Whichone might be superior: "The beautifully bred Whichone…is a better horse than he was in [the Belmont]…His victory in the Miller Stakes was a most impressive effort. The manner in which he trimmed the field, coupled with a swiftly run pace, indicates that he is in the peak of his form."[5]

The interest in the 1930 Travers was intense, with Whichone and Gallant Fox each having a win over the other. A torrential downpour did not deter the racing fans and Governor Franklin Delano Roosevelt from filling the Saratoga Race Course to capacity. Although no attendance records at racetracks were kept until after World War II, most writers estimated that the crowd that braved the rain was the largest in that track's history.

It proved to be a memorable event: Gallant Fox, the 1-2 favorite, engaged in a speed duel with Whichone, and when both faltered, Jim Dandy came splashing down the middle of the track to win by eight astonishing lengths. Unfortunately, Whichone bowed a tendon during the race, and although he bravely managed to cross the finish line ahead of the fourth-place horse, Sun Falcon, his promising career was over. Gallant Fox finished the year with wins in the Saratoga Cup, Lawrence Realization and Jockey Club Gold Cup, guaranteeing his future induction into the Hall of Fame, while Whichone was consigned to relative oblivion.

As is often the case, Whichone's brilliance on the track did not translate to success in the breeding shed. In his approximately thirteen years at stud, he only managed to get into the top twenty leading sires list of the *Daily Racing Form* twice, finishing eleventh in 1938 and sixteenth in 1939. Probably his most accomplished offspring was Handcuff—a filly out of the Friar Rock mare Tenez—the champion three-year-old filly of 1938 with wins in the Acorn, Delaware Oaks, Alabama and New England Oaks. The rest of her career, however, was undistinguished.

According to pedigreequery.com, Whichone died in 1944. If that date is correct, Whichone's passing was not noticed by either the *Blood-Horse* or the *American Racing Manual*, a fitting coda to what should have been a remarkable career.

Filly for the Course

Although most contemporary Saratoga race fans would consider Fourstardave the ultimate horse for the course, there was a late nineteenth-century California-based filly named Los Angeles who compiled a remarkable career record at Saratoga of eighteen wins, six places and one show out of twenty-five starts.

An 1885 foal, she was by Glenelg out of the Lexington mare La Polka. From the same crop that year were her stablemate and future Hall of Fame inductee Emperor of Norfolk, Raceland, Sir Dixon and Bella B. Los Angeles hasn't been elected to Hall of Fame yet, but her statistics show that she belongs in the conversation. She would run against all these contemporaries, male or female. Like all distaff runners of that time period, she would often run against the opposite sex in her first two years of racing and run exclusively in open company after her three-year-old season.

Los Angeles's owner was the legendary California horseman, gambler and businessman Elias Jackson "Lucky" Baldwin. Although he preferred racing his own homebreds, Los Angeles was a product of Dan Swigert's Elmendorf Farm in Kentucky and was purchased for $3,500.

Baldwin's home base was his Rancho Santa Anita, the present site of the Santa Anita Park racetrack, but his runners were hardly California provincials. Each spring, Baldwin brought his horses to the Midwest, continued on to Kentucky, New Jersey and New York and then wended their way back west, winding up in San Francisco.

ELIAS JACKSON BALDWIN, Founder

Elias "Lucky" Baldwin, owner of Los Angeles. *Courtesy of Bill Mochon.*

Los Angeles began her career in the spring of 1887 with three stakes wins at Churchill Downs. After an unsuccessful trip to St. Louis and Chicago, she regained her form by winning the Lassie and the open Tyro Stakes at Monmouth Park. She was now ready for her inaugural race at what was to be her favorite track, the historic Spinaway at Saratoga.

Although she faced six other two-year-old fillies with a less-than-daunting cumulative record of one win in twenty-four starts, she went off at what would seem like generous odds of 2-1. The wisdom of the bettors was affirmed, however, when she only won by a neck. After a side trip back to Monmouth, she returned to Saratoga to finish second in the Misses Stakes to 12-1 shot Geraldine. Los Angeles ended her first season at Saratoga with a win in the open Equity Stakes, beating the multiple stakes winner King Fish and avenging her earlier defeat to Geraldine, who finished fifth.

Following a rather disappointing spring and early summer of 1888 at Kentucky, Kansas City and New Jersey—her only significant win during that stretch was in the Monmouth Oaks—she returned to the restorative waters of the Spa to compete in the venerable Travers on opening day. She only faced two colts and another filly in that race, but one of those colts was the outstanding Sir Dixon, who, in addition to winning the Carlton, Withers and Belmont Stakes, had beaten Los Angeles three weeks earlier in the Lorillard at Monmouth.

Sir Dixon was made the 2-1 favorite, with Los Angeles the 3-1 second choice, and that is how the race ended, with Sir Dixon defeating Los Angeles by four lengths. Four days later, she was entered in the Alabama, which was, and still is, restricted to three-year-old fillies. She was made the favorite but finished second to Bella B., one of the best fillies of her generation and who would often contend against Los Angeles during their three- and four-year-old seasons. Los Angeles became the first horse to finish on the board in both the Alabama and Travers. Since then, four others have accomplished this feat: Lady Rotha (1915), Prudery (1921), Nimba (1927) and Chris Evert (1974). No filly has ever won both.

Los Angeles ended her 1888 season at Saratoga with three straight wins in the Foxhall (1⅝ miles), Kenner (2 miles) for three-year-olds and the Pocahontas (1 mile, 500 yards) for three-year-old fillies.

In 1889, Los Angeles began her season with three wins from seven starts and opened her stay at Saratoga by finishing second to Princess Dowling in the Adirondack Handicap. She went off at odds of 7-1 and conceded twelve pounds to the winner, a three-year-old filly that was the second choice at 5-2. The 8-5 favorite, King Crab, finished third, and her familiar opponent Bella B. finished fourth.

Three days later, she won the 1¼-mile Excelsior, which was up to that date the most impressive win of her career. Finishing second was future Hall of Famer Hanover. Although critics could point out that Hanover was not the same horse as he was two years ago, he still managed to win the Coney Island Cup (beating Firenze), the Coney Island Handicap (beating Kingston) and the California at Saratoga before losing to Los Angeles in the Excelsior. Factors that contributed to the filly's win were Hanover's obvious dislike for the sloppy track and the twelve-pound weight advantage she was given. Nevertheless, a win over Hanover was a significant addition to her résumé.

Standout Hanover was beaten a neck in the 1889 Excelsior. *Courtesy of the National Museum of Racing.*

As was often her custom, Los Angeles left Saratoga for a brief visit to the Jersey shore, where she won a free handicap and then beat Firenze, another future Hall of Famer, in the Champion Stakes. Thus, in a one-week period, Los Angeles defeated two future Hall of Fame inductees. After an eleven-day rest, she concluded her 1889 Saratoga season with the first of three consecutive wins in the Congress Hall. This peculiar race was a throwback to an earlier time, since the winner had to win two of three six-furlong heats. Los Angeles never lost a heat in her three wins in the Congress Hall.

In 1890, she had her worst start of her career, losing six of her first seven starts, her only win coming in an allowance race at Chicago's Washington Park. One of her losses was a last place to ten other rivals in the New York Jockey Club Handicap at Morris Park.

Remarkably, 1890 was to be the best season of her career at Saratoga, where she reversed her dismal start by winning six out of seven stakes. After opening her Saratoga meet with a win in the California, she ran what might have been the greatest race of her career in the 1¼-mile Excelsior. She only

Hall of Famer Kingston couldn't handle Lucky Baldwin's filly. *Courtesy of the National Museum of Racing.*

faced two horses, but one was the future Hall of Famer Kingston, who lost by a length to Los Angeles despite receiving three pounds from her. Finishing third and last by ten lengths was Teuton, an invader from the West that had earlier beaten Los Angeles in the Oakwood and Wheeler Handicaps at Washington Park.

Los Angeles' other stakes wins that summer at Saratoga were in the Kearney, Merchants', Beverwyck and Congress Hall. Her only loss was a second to Lavinia Belle in the Hotel Balmoral. She conceded twelve pounds to that filly and had earlier beaten her in the Merchants' Stakes, and five days after the Hotel Balmoral, she defeated her in the Beverwyck.

When Los Angeles began her 1891 season in New York, it was obvious that she had passed her prime. With only two wins from her first eleven starts, both purse events, she would need the usual Saratoga elixir to recapture her lost glory. She only won one of her first three races at her favorite track, including her worst finish there, a third in an $800 purse event, but eventually whatever it was about Saratoga that made her a star finally took effect. She won her last four races at Saratoga, ending her career with her third Congress Hall, a walkover in the Morrissey and a victory over two overmatched rivals in the prestigious Saratoga Cup. There could not have been a more appropriate end for Saratoga's female horse for the course.

Some statistics may help describe her affinity for Saratoga. Until her final season in 1891, all her starts at Saratoga were in stakes. Except for two purse wins in 1891, all her wins were in stakes, and her record of sixteen stakes wins at Saratoga is a record that is likely to last forever. In her twenty-five starts at Saratoga, she was never off the board, and her only show occurred in a purse race in 1891. Only four of her Saratoga races were exclusively against fillies.

A Pair of Dead-Heat Travers

Though separated by 138 years, the Travers of 1874 and 2012 are connected by a total of four noses on the wire, which produced the only two dead-heat finishes in Saratoga's oldest stakes.

In the 11th Travers, the stewards decided that Atilla and Acrobat reached the finish line together, just ahead of another horse that some observers felt was the winner. Thanks to a precise digital photo-finish camera, there was no doubt that favored Alpha was able to catch long shot Golden Ticket at precisely the right fraction of a second to produce a rare tie for the victory in the 143rd Travers. That race also had another horse in the picture, Fast Falcon, who was a neck back.

Since runoffs were often used to decide dead heats in the nineteenth century, Atilla is considered the official winner of the 1874 running. Alpha and Golden Ticket will forever be a part of Saratoga Race Course history as the first dual winners of the race. Both races had eleven-horse fields that lacked major stars, but they produced dramatic finishes that stunned the crowds each of those days.

Acrobat, by Lexington out of the Glencoe mare Sally Lewis, was bred by A.J. Alexander's Woodburn Stud in Kentucky and originally owned by H.P. McGrath. Unraced as a two-year-old, he finished third in his first race, Monmouth Park's Ocean Hotel Stakes on July 15, 1874. The winner of that race was Aaron Pennington, who had previously won the Phoenix Hotel at Lexington Park. Three days later, Acrobat won Monmouth Park's Robins Stakes under the new ownership of K.W. Sears and Dan Swigert.

Golden Ticket, on the inside, and Alpha hit the wire together to finish in a dead heat for the win in the 2012 Travers. *Photo by Mike Kane.*

Finishing second in that race was Aaron Pennington. After the Travers, Acrobat finished second to Stampede in the Kenner at Saratoga and ended his three-year-old season by winning the Jerome and a purse race at Jerome Park. Thoroughbred Heritage named him the 1874 champion three-year-old male.

According to turf historian Walter Vosburgh, Acrobat was afflicted with shelly feet and soles throughout his career,[6] which account for his sparse record of two races in 1875 and three in 1876. Although he only won one race in 1876, the Centennial at Monmouth Park, his two losses that year were seconds to multiple stakes winner Tom Ochiltree.

Atilla (also spelled Attila) was by Australian out of the Lexington mare Ultima. He was also bred by A.J. Alexander and was owned by Pierre Lorillard. Like Acrobat, he did not race as a two-year-old, and the Travers was the third and last race of his career, retiring undefeated. He began his 1874 season on June 20 by winning a purse race for three-year-olds that had not won a race that year. His second race, a purse event on July 11 at Morris Park, was a win against older horses. Among the also-rans were Survivor, who would later win the Fordham Cup; five-year-old Woodbine, the first winner of the Alabama in 1872 and who would later win the Long Branch at Monmouth; and Vandalia, that year's champion three-year-old filly that would later win the Annual Sweepstakes at Monmouth Park and the Dixie and Breckenridge at Pimlico.

The 1874 Travers was run at the same 1¾-mile distance that had been the norm since that stake's first running in 1864. Although there was no clear favorite throughout most of the betting, a late surge made Atilla the slight favorite just before the start of the race. The field was the largest in the Travers's short history.

According to the *New York Times* account of the race, when the field reached the half-mile pole, the leaders were Rutherford and Stampede, with Brigand a close third. When the horses hit the finish line, however, it appeared to the *Times* reporter that Steel Eyes had won the race by a head, with Acrobat and Atilla tied for second and third.[7] However, the stewards, who obviously did not have the benefit of a photo-finish image to review, declared the race a dead heat between Atilla and Acrobat, with Steel Eyes a close third.

The Monday edition of the *New York Times* reiterated the opinion that Steel Eyes had won the race.[8] The *Spirit of the Times* saw nothing controversial about the judges' decision.[9] The correspondents for the *Yankee Clipper*[10] and the *New York Daily Tribune*[11] noted that most of the spectators thought that Steel Eyes had won. The time was a fast 3:09 1/2.

As was the custom of the time with dead heats, if both owners consented, a runoff was held after the conclusion of that day's card. The distance was the same 1¾ miles. Although Acrobat set the pace for most of the race, Atilla, the favorite at $1,000 to $700, prevailed after taking the lead at the homestretch, winning by three-quarters of a length. Remarkably, the time of 3:08 3/4 was three-quarters of a second faster than the previous race and within half a second of Joe Daniels's record for the distance.

The race proved to be a costly victory for Atilla, as he pulled up lame after the runoff and never raced again. Bad feet limited Acrobat to only five races in the 1875 and 1876 seasons, and according to Vosburgh, he died an "early death."[12]

Alpha, a Darley homebred by Bernardini out of the Nijinsky II mare Munnaya, had won the Jim Dandy earlier in the meet and was the 2-1 favorite. He had debuted with a maiden victory at Saratoga on September 3, 2011, and reached the Travers with four wins and two seconds in six races at New York tracks. His two starts outside the state were a pair of clunkers at Churchill Downs: eleventh in the 2011 Breeders' Cup Juvenile and a twelfth in the 2012 Kentucky Derby.

Golden Ticket, a Speightstown colt out of the Deputy Minister mare Business Plan, had a far less impressive résumé. His lone win in nine starts was in a maiden special weight race on February 11 at Gulfstream Park, and trainer Kenny McPeek opted to try the $1 million Travers only after two races he had targeted did not have enough entries to be used. Golden Ticket had some stakes experience, finishing second in the Tampa Bay Derby and fifth in the Coolmore Lexington Stakes. The Travers on August 25 was his first start since a second in an allowance race on May 5, and he was 33-1 in the Travers betting.

The ownership groups were decidedly different, too. Alpha was owned by Godolphin, the international racing powerhouse operated by the ruling family of Dubai. Golden Ticket carried the colors of Magic City

The owners, trainers and jockeys of Golden Ticket and Alpha celebrate their dead-heat finish in the crowded winner's circle. *Photo by Mike Kane.*

Thoroughbred Partners, a small group from Billings, Montana, that was in its second season.

Alpha and Golden Ticket were in stalking positions, a couple of lengths behind Speightscity through six furlongs in 1:12.62. Jockey David Cohen took Golden Ticket up the rail approaching the quarter pole and held a one-length advantage with a sixteenth of a mile to go. Alpha and jockey Ramon Dominguez were a bit wider but kept coming, and the colt got his nose up at the right time as the pair hit the wire in 2:02.74.

No one was sure who won, and track announcer Tom Durkin couldn't make the call. While photo-finish camera operator Don Morehouse and the placing judges looked at the image on the computer screen, the crowd of 46,528 caught its breath and applauded.

"I thought we were second-best at the sixteenth pole," said Alpha's trainer, Kiaran McLaughlin. "I didn't think we were going to get there, and then the last lunge or two I thought maybe we got there. The photo indicated a tie, and we'll take it."

McPeek was pleased to share the top prize: "First I thought we won, then I thought we lost and I looked at it again—nobody could tell. I was happy for Kiaran, too. We've known each other since we were kids."[13]

The owners, trainers and jockeys celebrated together in the winner's circle, and the New York Racing Association placed two canoes painted in the colors of the Travers winners in the infield lake.

Alpha and Golden Ticket met again in the Pennsylvania Derby at Parx, with Golden Ticket finishing third and Alpha sixth. In their final starts of the year, Golden Ticket was eleventh in the Hollywood Derby and Alpha twelfth in the Breeders' Cup Classic at Santa Anita.

Travers Trainer Mary Hirsch Stands Alone

T railblazer Mary Hirsch captured the 1938 Travers with her very first starter in the race, and seventy-five years later, she is the only female trainer to win Saratoga's oldest and most famous event.

Thanksgiving's four-length victory in a race that did not have a bearing on the three-year-old male championship could have been forgettable, but it has a place in the rich history of Saratoga Race Course. A few women have saddled Travers horses in the last thirty years, but none has matched Hirsch's achievement.

By the time Thanksgiving defeated a field of nine on August 13, 1938, Hirsch was quite used to stepping into territory that had not been open to women. She was the first female to receive a license from The Jockey Club, although it took a while; the first to saddle a horse in the Kentucky Derby; and the first to win a stakes race at Saratoga, the 1936 Diana Handicap.

Racing was, after all, the Hirsch family business. Her father, Max, and brother, Buddy, were high-profile trainers who would be elected to the Hall of Fame, and another brother, Max Jr., was a successful trainer who died in an automobile accident in 1950.

Since her family lived in a cottage on the grounds of Belmont Park, Hirsch grew up around horses and learned how to handle them from one of the sport's all-time greats. Although she had the pedigree and firsthand experience, it took her more than two years to obtain a license from The Jockey Club, which controlled racing in New York and was important nationally.

Pioneering female trainer Mary Hirsch won the 1938 Travers. *Courtesy of the Keeneland Library.*

In early 1933, three years after leaving boarding school and beginning to work as an assistant to her father, Hirsch formally applied for a license. The *New York Times* gave the story substantial coverage.[14] "A 20-year-old girl has thrown a bombshell into that exclusive company of 50 gentlemen, most of whom are well past the half-century mark and who guide the destinies of the Jockey Club," Bryan Field wrote. "The Jockey Club is the governing body of the turf in New York State and yesterday there came into its offices the first application in its history from a woman for a license as trainer."

Hirsch told Field that she intended to follow in the footsteps of her famous father but outside of the considerable shadow that he cast. "She wants her own place in the sun and has filed application for a license to train for the very simple reason that she believes she can train because she has trained thoroughbreds."[15]

Hirsch owned a two-year-old filly named Tullihoo that she intended to train in her own name. Her goal was to have the filly compete at the Havre de Grace track in Maryland. While Hirsch was a skilled horseman, she told Field that she had no interest in being a jockey.

Algernon Daingerfield, assistant secretary and assistant treasurer of The Jockey Club, said that Hirsch's application would be considered. However, Daingerfield noted in the *Times* story that the masculine pronoun "he" in important rule no. 209 seemed to indicate that the rules excluded women. Hirsch was not granted a license in 1933 because the matter was tabled, but in July 1934, the Illinois Racing Commission approved her application.[16] Michigan also gave her a license.

In April 1935, The Jockey Club granted a license that practically opened the door for her to train everywhere in the United States and Europe.[17] The

New York Times article noted that Hirsch had arranged to train the horses owned by Bernard Baruch and others that had been in her father's stable. By then, it was understood that Hirsch was actively training horses running in her father's name.[18]

The *American Racing Manual*, published by *Daily Racing Form*, shows Hirsch winning ten races and her horses earning $10,365 in purse money in 1935. She improved on those numbers in 1936 with seventeen winners and $18,575. One of those wins came with No Sir in the Diana at Saratoga Race Course. Finishing second at 4-5 was that year's champion two-year-old colt Pompoon. In those days, the Diana was a race for female owners. She doubled up as the owner and trainer.[19]

Hirsch ran No Sir in the 1937 Kentucky Derby, where he finished thirteenth in the field of twenty. Meanwhile, Max Hirsch was training the two-year-old Thanksgiving for Mrs. Parker Corning. The colt by Bud Lerner out of the Inchcape mare Inchcape Belle won two of five starts that season and did not race again after finishing sixth of twelve in the Albany Handicap at Saratoga.

Mrs. Corning's husband was a six-term congressman who represented his hometown of Albany, New York, from 1923 to 1937.[20] Congressman Corning's grandfather, Erastus Corning, was the first president of the New York Central Railroad, and his nephew, also named Erastus, was the mayor of Albany for forty years.

In a 1937 feature story in the *Schenectady Gazette* that described Hirsch as "pretty, dark, vivacious," Hirsch joked about breaking stereotypes: "People are usually surprised that I do not chew tobacco."[21]

Thanksgiving returned to competition in 1938 in Mary Hirsch's care. He was second in his first start at Jamaica on April 16 and then was a well-beaten sixth a week later at Havre de Grace. Under jockey Jack Westrope, he was second in the Withers at Belmont Park on May 21 and picked up his first victory of the season in the Constitution Handicap at Suffolk Downs in Boston on May 28. Facing stiffer competition in Suffolk's Yankee Handicap, he was third carrying top weight in a race in which Cravat broke the track record.

Hirsch brought him back to New York, and he ran well in a pair of losses at Empire City. Santa Anita Derby winner Stagehand, who had beaten Seabiscuit and other older horses in the Santa Anita Handicap, won the first race, the Empire City Handicap, in track-record time. Thanksgiving was asked to cut back to seven furlongs in his first start of the season and was beaten by a head by Airflame in the American Legion Handicap. He ended

Eddie Arcaro guided Thanksgiving to a wire-to-wire victory. *Courtesy of the Keeneland Library.*

his four-race losing streak with a ten-length victory in the Saranac Handicap four days later.

After running four times in twenty days in July, Thanksgiving was given a couple of weeks off before the Travers. The field was led by Stagehand; Bull Lea, who had won the Kenner and would go on to be the sire of seven Hall of Fame members; and Arlington Classic winner Nedayr. Absent were Derby winner Lawrin, Preakness winner Dauber and Belmont Stakes winner Pastuerized. Thanksgiving was assigned 117 pounds, 10 less than Stagehand and Nedayr in the allowance conditions in effect.

Eddie Arcaro was aboard Thanksgiving, replacing regular rider Lucas Dupps, and he guided the colt to a wire-to-wire victory. In *American Race Horses, 1938*, the writer John Hervey said, "Thanksgiving, ridden by Eddie Arcaro, took the track at the fall of the flag and made all the others look common, leading all the way and winning fairly in a canter by four lengths." Thanksgiving completed the mile and a quarter in 2:03 3/5, the fastest time for the race since Man o' War tied the track record of 2:01 2/5 in 1920.

Mrs. Parker Corning's Thanksgiving reaches the wire four lengths ahead of the competition. *Courtesy of the Keeneland Library*.

Two weeks later, Thanksgiving won the Huron Handicap by a length to complete his stay at Saratoga with three wins and a second in major stakes. Thanksgiving finished off the board in two stakes at Narragansett Park won by Stagehand, later named the three-year-old male champion, and was given the rest of the year off. He won four of thirteen races in 1938 and earned $35,925 in purses.

Hirsch's Travers victory didn't receive any special attention in the press reports of the race; the *New York Times* reported that the colt was trained by Max Hirsch.

In 1939, Thanksgiving won two of his seven stakes starts; he was second in the Merchants' and Citizens' Handicap at Saratoga and earned $22,725. Hirsch sent out a personal-best twenty-nine winners in what was her fifth and final season as a trainer. She retired that winter and on March 31, 1940, married Charles McLennan, the racing secretary at prominent tracks Hialeah, Keeneland and Pimlico.[22]

Nineteenth-Century Steeplechasing and Hurdles Racing

Today, the terms "hurdles" and "steeplechasing" are interchangeable, but in the nineteenth century, there were distinct differences between the two types of racing events.

Hurdle races were held on the main dirt track, and the only obstacles were temporary wooden fences. Steeplechase races, on the other hand, were run on the grass infield and dirt courses. They consisted of many different obstacles, such as fences, water and bushes, and they tended to meander in no particular set pattern rather than the oval dirt courses used for hurdle racing. In fact, steeplechase races in England were originally run through the countryside, and the term came from one of the most prominent landmarks used in these events.

Hurdle races in Saratoga Springs are older than the track itself. A short item in the 1858 *American Turf Register and Racing and Trotting Calendar* reported on a two-day meet that consisted of a two-mile hurdle race with a purse of $200 "over eight hurdles three feet six inches high, stiff timber" on September 17, as well as a one-mile hurdle race with a purse of $75 and a one-mile race, presumably on the flats, on September 18.[23]

The field for the hurdle race on the first day consisted of three horses: Charley Reilly, the winner, whose name can be found in print spelled in different ways; Lady Franklin; and Harkaway, who bolted. The first two horses competed in the second day's events, with Charley Reilly winning the hurdles again and Lady Franklin winning the flat race. Harkaway, who misbehaved the day before, was presumably banished in disgrace.

Map of the 1880s Saratoga steeplechase course. *Courtesy of the Saratoga Room, Saratoga Springs Public Library.*

Although the site of that event was never mentioned, most likely it was held at either the Old Trotting Track, later called Horse Haven, or the newly built Richmond Trotting Course, which was located on Lake Avenue about three-quarters of a mile east of the Saratoga Springs village limits.

John Morrissey and his partners' new Saratoga Race Course opened on August 2, 1864, and that track's first hurdle race was the first event run on the fourth day of the meet, August 6. The distance was two miles over eight hurdles. The *New York Herald* reported that "[t]he hurdle race…was a novel and highly attractive feature, and one which created the most intense excitement among the assembled thousands while it was in progress."[24] Similarly, the *Daily Saratogian* stated that "[t]he race was an exciting one, such interest being manifested to see race horses leap tall hurdles 3 1-2 feet high, with grown men on their backs."[25]

The chart for that inaugural hurdle race lists only the order of finish for the five horses, which was typical for charts at that time. Missing was the excitement that accompanied the race. The favorite, Zigzag, led for most of the race, with Charley Reilly, who had participated in that 1858 two-day meeting, coming from last to engage the leader before the last hurdle. That last obstacle proved to be the undoing of Zigzag, who fell, with Charley Reilly also falling after becoming entangled with Zigzag. Garryowen cleared both the last hurdle and the two fallen horses and assumed a clear lead for the finish line. Remarkably, Charley Reilly's jockey, McLaughlin, remounted and was able to press the leader without the use of a bridle, finishing second in the race, with Rescue third, Wild Irishman fourth and Zigzag last.

There were also interesting subplots in that race. All the horses were based in Canada, which is not surprising, since Canadians had been holding jumping races for a quarter of a century before their cousins to the south began running them on a regular basis. All five horses had faced each other numerous times, including a hurdle race held one week earlier on the St. Maurice Course in Three Rivers, Quebec, with Garryowen finishing first, Wild Irishman second and Zigzag third, with two others falling. There is no apparent reason why the bettors at Saratoga made Zigzag the favorite despite the result of the previous race.

In addition, there is the "Charley Reilly returns to Saratoga" angle. Although the *Daily Saratogian* described him as eighteen years old,[26] the *American Turf Register* account of the 1858 races listed him as being nine years old,[27] which, if true, would "only" make him fifteen at the time of the 1864 race. There is no way of verifying his age, since he is not listed in The Jockey Club's first *American Stud Book*, and the charts do not give the name of his dam, but he was nevertheless a remarkably durable athlete.

Zigzag brushed off his fall in 1864 and returned to Saratoga to win the only hurdle race held there in 1865, as well as the two that were held in 1866. He had a highly successful campaign in 1866, winning thirteen of eighteen races, with three seconds and two thirds. His record that year would have been more impressive if not for the presence of a mare named Nannie Craddock, who accounted for three of his defeats. Zigzag defeated that rival in five of their encounters, the last win ending tragically when Nannie Craddock had to be humanely destroyed after breaking her leg in a steeplechase handicap at the Montreal Hunt Club on November 1. Zigzag started five times in 1867, his last season, finishing second in all his races, including two at Saratoga.

On June 7, 1865, Paterson, New Jersey, hosted the first steeplechase race in America. Some familiar names were entered in that race. The winner was the ill-fated Nannie Craddock, the place horse was her constant rival and Saratoga favorite Zigzag and third was the ageless Charley Reilly, who at that time was either nineteen or sixteen.

Steeplechasing became very popular in the United States, and on October 26, 1869, Jerome Park held "the first running of a true Steeplechase at a major race track."[28] The winner was Oysterman jr., who, with Zigzag, became one of the first steeplechase favorites at Saratoga. On July 15, 1870, the Saratoga Association unveiled its new steeplechase course. It was officially described as "about three miles over a fair hunting course."[29] According to Peter Winants, "The course wound about the infield, then crossed the dirt track on the backstretch to pass through what now is a stable area."[30] A description in the *Spirit of the Times* of a steeplechase event on August 13 gives a good idea of the steeplechase course:

The start was in the field behind the judges' stand. At the stonewall Raven led...The same order was preserved at the next fence...So they took a wall and a fence near the lower turn. They now bent towards the stand and cleared a wall, then a brush fence, and then the longest leap, the hedge and water near the stand...They then jumped two fences and [sic] into the lower field, and then encountered a stone wall...Coursing through the field they jumped two fences near the quarter pole and into the outer field...In front of the stables they had two jumps, the first a fence and the second a stone wall. They now ran to the right close up to the far fence, and then wheeling jumped a fence; then they ran out of the field across the regular track, over two fences on either side of the fractional track and into the north field...They ran then to the north and jumped a hedge and then a fence topped with brush; turning, they dashed up a stone wall and took it flying...They now came to the water jump in front of the stand and took it flying...When they entered the regular track at the half-mile pole there were two hurdles between them and home.[31]

The winner of the track's first steeplechase event was also Oysterman jr. His steeplechase record in his first season at Saratoga was three wins and one place from five starts. His only off-the-board race occurred on July 19 when he fell at the sixth hurdle while in the lead. Before coming to Saratoga for the 1871 season, he won the prestigious Grand National Steeplechase at Monmouth Park. His two wins in two races at Saratoga were so dominant that the *New York Times*, perhaps with tongue in cheek, complained that he was "an almost invariable winner...The triumphs of Oysterman, jr. have got to be monotonous, if not irksome."[32] Oysterman jr. did not race at Saratoga after his 1871 season, giving him a record of five wins and one place from seven starts at the upstate track.

In 1871, the steeplechase course, whose distance was described as $2\frac{3}{4}$ miles, was changed to incorporate shorter races. Fractional course no. 1 was about $2\frac{1}{4}$ miles, and fractional course no. 2 was about $1\frac{1}{2}$ miles.

The popularity of jumping events was discussed in an 1871 article in the *New York Times*: "Among the sports of the turf which have lately become so popular, hurdle racing is pre-eminently the favorite. So marked is the preference for this pastime, that on the days when it is announced on the programmes of race-meetings the attendance is almost invariably increased."[33] An indication of the popularity of jumping events in general at the Spa was the dramatic increase in such races through the years. In 1870, there were two races on the new steeplechase course and three hurdle

Drawing from the *Daily Graphic*, August 14, 1877. Neither horse was injured. *Courtesy of the Saratoga Room, Saratoga Springs Public Library.*

events during the twelve-day meet. There were usually five or six races a day. By 1877, there were five steeplechase races and four hurdle events during the twenty-one-day meet. In 1882, there were twelve steeplechase races and seven hurdle races during the thirty-five-day meet. Both steeplechasing and hurdle races were discontinued from 1889 through 1891 but were resumed in 1892.

Although most, if not all, of the nation's top steeplechase stars raced at Saratoga, the best might have been an 1870 foal by Ulverston out of Kate McDonald named Trouble. Like most steeplechasers, Trouble showed little ability on the flats before being converted to a jumper. He did not race as a two-year-old and was winless on two starts in 1873 before beginning his career as a jumper with four wins from as many starts in 1874. In his nine-year steeplechase/hurdles career, Trouble started fifty-six times, winning thirty-eight, finishing second fifteen times and finishing out of the money only three times.

In his three off-the board races, one occurred when he won the race easily but was disqualified when his jockey, Murphy, dismounted before receiving permission from the stewards. The second occurred when he fell, and the third happened at Saratoga in 1876 when he finished fourth after conceding fifteen, eighteen and twenty-seven pounds to the first three finishers. His record at Saratoga was fifteen wins and eight seconds from twenty-five starts. He won the following stakes: the 1874 and 1877 Grand National Steeplechase Handicap at Jerome Park, the 1875 Steeplechase Post Stakes at Pimlico, the 1875 Long Branch Grand National Steeplechase at Monmouth, the first running of the Trouble Steeplechase in 1881 and the North American Steeplechase at Saratoga. The last two occurred when he was eleven years old. In the last race of his career, the 1882 Trouble Stakes at Saratoga, he finished second by one length to Postguard while conceding five pounds to that opponent. It was the only stakes race he ever lost.

Although today's steeplechase races are not popular with Saratoga's betting public or, for that reason, racing officials, it is worth noting that this was not always the case.

Leading Jockeys and Trainers, 1900-1959

B lack signs with gold letters welcome visitors to Saratoga Springs, with the motto "Health, History, Horses." While Saratoga Race Course is a historic venue, huge chunks of statistical information about the races that took place on the grounds prior to the late 1950s was not available for many years. That has changed and is being published for the first time here.

The data tables show the leading jockeys since 1900 and the leading trainers since 1902, the first year that the name of the winning trainer appeared in charts of races. Among the revelations: brilliant young jockey Walter Miller won thirty-three races in twenty-two days in 1907, Laverne Fator rode thirty-seven winners during the twenty-seven-day meeting in 1921 and trainer Sam Hildreth's record twenty victories in 1922 was equaled twice in the 1990s but wasn't broken until 2001 when Bill Mott saddled twenty-two winners.

The New York Racing Association, which had just been formed as the Greater New York Racing Association, purchased Saratoga Race Course in 1955 and has operated the meet at the nation's oldest track since 1956. Through the years, NYRA's media guide has contained data about Saratoga racing since 1958. Who were the leading jockeys and trainers in the summers prior to then was anyone's guess.

That shortcoming, a shroud over Saratoga's past, made it difficult to put accomplishments in perspective. Much more of that history is now recorded, thanks to the work of Joe Peck, Jim Sweet and Bill Cavanagh, three research volunteers during the 2000s at the National Museum of Racing.

In 2006, Peck accepted an assignment from Mike Kane, then the communications officer at the museum, to start compiling the pre-NYRA stats at Saratoga. Using *Daily Racing Form* chart books, Peck began the tedious task of documenting the daily results of the 1946 season when Saratoga reopened following World War II. Sweet and Cavanagh heard about the project in 2007, joined the team and began filling up legal pads with the names of the winning horses, their owners, trainers, jockeys and margins of victory. In their journey through charts to the end of the 2000 season, Peck, Sweet and Cavanagh also noted special accomplishments, such as a horse returning a day or two after a victory to win again and victories by apprentices.

With twenty-two winners in 2001, Bill Mott broke Samuel Hildreth's single-season record of twenty victories set in 1922. *Photo by Mike Kane.*

Kane came up with the idea for the research when the NYRA press office inquired about records for apprentice riders at Saratoga. There was no way to say that Julien Leparoux's twenty-eight wins that summer was a record for an apprentice. The expanded statistics now show that Leparoux's win total is the record for meets run since 1900.

Jimmy McTaggart was the first of three apprentices to win a riding title at Saratoga when he recorded twenty-three winners in twenty-six racing days in 1913. Silvio Coucci led the way in 1932 with twenty-three wins in thirty racing days. John Ruane tied with Bobby Ussery at seventeen for the top spot in the twenty-four-day meet in 1957.

In 2003, when Todd Pletcher was piling up victories en route to the third of his nine training titles through 2012, the media, using the NYRA media guide, tracked how Pletcher was closing in on Sylvester Veitch's record of twenty-four wins in 1954. Journalist Bill Mooney decided to take a look at the chart books and discovered that Veitch had nineteen winners, not twenty-four. Pletcher actually broke Mott's record of twenty-two set two years earlier on his way to thirty-five. Pletcher and Mott share the Saratoga record with nine titles.

Above: Jockey Angel Cordero Jr. leaps off the back of another winner at Saratoga. Cordero won fourteen riding titles at the Spa. *Courtesy of the National Museum of Racing*

Left: Sunny Jim Fitzsimmons trained at Saratoga for more than sixty years, and the first and last of his four meet titles were thirty-two years apart. *Courtesy of the Maryland Jockey Club.*

Fator's record, which stood until 1959, when Manny Ycaza rode forty-one winners, came at a time when a Saratoga program consisted of six races. He had at least one winner in twenty-three of the twenty-seven days and won fourteen stakes, including the Miller and the Alabama.

Ted Atkinson won five riding titles and Fator and Eddie Arcaro four each as they built their Hall of Fame résumés. Angel Cordero Jr. came along in the 1960s, winning in 1967 the first of his fourteen titles—eleven of them in a row—and was properly dubbed the "King of Saratoga."

Miller was a phenom and dominated the sport for about five years before he grew and added pounds, which forced a move to Europe, where he could ride at higher weights. In 1906, Miller's meet-leading 26 winners were part of 388 wins for the season, a national record that stood until 1952. Miller's 33 wins at Saratoga in 1907 included ten stakes.

Hildreth was the leading trainer six times in eighteen meets held between 1910 and 1929. Sunny Jim Fitzsimmons, who twice trained Triple Crown winners, was the leading trainer at Saratoga four times: 1930, 1934, 1950 and in 1962, his last full year of training, when he was eighty-eight.

1900s Leading Jockeys and Trainers

Year	Racing Days	Jockey	Wins	Trainer	Wins
1900	22	Tommy Burns	20	No records available. Winning trainers not listed on charts of races.	
1901	22	Willie Shaw	20		
1902	22	Arthur Redfern	20	John Madden	11
1903	22	Grover C. Fuller	23	James Rowe Sr.	11
1904	22	Eugene Hildebrand	16	H.H. Hyner	10
1905	22	Willie Knapp	11	H.H. Hyner	7
1906	22	Walter Miller	26	John W. Rogers	7
				John Madden	8
				Tom Welsh	8
1907	22	Walter Miller	33	William Hayward Jr.	12
1908	15	Carroll Schilling	25	John Madden	16
1909	24	Charles Grand	11	Thomas J. Healey	8
		James Davenport	11		

1910s LEADING JOCKEYS AND TRAINERS

Year	Racing Days	Jockey	Wins	Trainer	Wins
1910	24	Carroll Schilling	20	Sam Hildreth	16
1911		No racing at Saratoga due to gambling ban in New York.			
1912					
1913	26	James McTaggart	23	John A. Mayberry	13
1914	25	James Butwell	16	James Rowe Sr.	10
				Thomas J. Healey	10
1915	24	Mack Garner	18	John F. Schorr	8
1916	24	James McTaggart	19	James Rowe Sr.	7
				Sam Hildreth	7
1917	26	James Butwell	13	Thomas J. Healey	12
1918	27	Frank Robinson	19	H. Guy Bedwell	7
				Thomas J. Healey	7
1919	26	Lavelle Ensor	14	William H. Karrick	13

1920s LEADING JOCKEYS AND TRAINERS

Year	Racing Days	Jockey	Wins	Trainer	Wins
1920	26	Frank Keogh	11	James Rowe Sr.	10
1921	27	Laverne Fator	37	James Rowe Sr.	10
1922	27	Laverne Fator	21	Sam Hildreth	20
1923	26	Linus McAtee	21	William Garth	13
1924	26	John Maiben	15	Sam Hildreth	9
1925	26	B. Thompson	12	Thomas J. Healey	8
1926	26	Earle Sande	19	G. Hamilton Keene	9
1927	30	Laverne Fator	20	Sam Hildreth	15
1928	30	Laverne Fator	17	Robert Smith	10
1929	27	Mack Garner	9	Sam Hildreth	15
		John Maiben	9		

1930s LEADING JOCKEYS AND TRAINERS

Year	Racing Days	Jockey	Wins	Trainer	Wins
1930	28	Sonny Workman	17	James Fitzsimmons	9
				George M. Odom	9
1931	27	Sonny Workman	12	James Rowe Jr.	10
1932	30	Silvio Coucci	23	William Brennan	10
1933	27	John Gilbert	18	William Brennan	10
				Robert Smith	10
1934	30	Don Meade	28	James Fitzsimmons	15
1935	30	Silvio Coucci	16	Joseph Stotler	8
				P.M. Walker	8
1936	28	Eddie Litzenberger	16	George Phillips	19
		James Stout	16		
1937	30	Eddie Arcaro	17	Hirsch Jacobs	9
1938	30	Eddie Arcaro	25	Frank Kearns	8
1939	30	John Longden	23	Bert Mulholland	15

1940s LEADING JOCKEYS AND TRAINERS

Year	Racing Days	Jockey	Wins	Trainer	Wins
1940	30	John Longden	21	Ben Jones	9
		Eddie Arcaro	21	Bert Mulholland	9
1941	30	Don Meade	27	John Gaver	9
1942	30	Conn McCreary	32	John Gaver	14
1943					
1944	No racing at Saratoga due to World War II travel restrictions.				
1945					
1946	24	Conn McCreary	19	Hirsch Jacobs	13
1947	24	Ted Atkinson	22	Horatio Luro	12
1948	24	Ted Atkinson	35	George P. Odom	8
1949	24	Ted Atkinson	26	Preston M. Burch	13

1950s LEADING JOCKEYS AND TRAINERS

YEAR	RACING DAYS	JOCKEY	WINS	TRAINER	WINS
1950	24	Eddie Arcaro	26	James Fitzsimmons	10
				Bert Mulholland	10
1951	24	Eric Guerin	25	John Gaver	16
1952	24	Ted Atkinson	24	William C. Winfrey	10
1953	24	Hedley Woodhouse	23	Sylvester Veitch	18
1954	24	Hedley Woodhouse	28	Sylvester Veitch	19
1955	24	Hedley Woodhouse	25	Sylvester Veitch	11
1956	24	Ted Atkinson	24	Hirsch Jacobs	9
1957	24	John Ruane	17	H. Allen Jerkens	8
		Robert Ussery	17		
1958	24	Bill Boland	22	Hirsch Jacobs	11
1959	24	Manuel Ycaza	41	Norman McLeod	8

A History of the Flash Stakes

The Flash Stakes, originally run in 1869, was the oldest race for two-year-olds in the country until its temporary suspension and final season at Saratoga after the 1971 meeting. For many years, it was the feature race on the opening-day program.

Charts of the Flash contain the names of racing's greats. Hall of Fame horses that won the Flash Stakes include Duke of Magenta, who broke his maiden in the 1871 running; Hamburg (1897); Sysonby (1904); Peter Pan (1906); Fair Play (1907); Old Rosebud (1913); Gallant Fox, with his maiden-breaker in 1929; Eight Thirty (1938); Assault, at odds of 70-1 in 1945, when the race was held at Belmont Park; Native Dancer (1952); and Riva Ridge (1971).

Some Hall of Fame horses were also-rans in the Flash: Parole (1875, fourth), Luke Blackburn (1879, fourth), Miss Woodford (1882, third) and Johnstown (1938, fourth).

Other champions that won the Flash were Remorseless (1869), Olitipa (1874), Zoo Zoo (1876), Harold (1878), Sensation (1879), George Kinney (1882), Burgomaster (1905), Billy Kelly (1918), Miss Jemina (1919) and Jamestown (1930).

From 1869 through 1901, the Flash was run at a distance of four furlongs, except for 1872, when its distance was six furlongs. From 1902 through 1968, it was run at 5½ furlongs. Its distance was six furlongs from 1969 through 1971, as well as during the years it was held at Belmont Park in the late 1980s and early in the twenty-first century.

Above: Old Rosebud before winning the Flash on opening day, 1913. *Courtesy of the National Museum of Racing.*

Below: Hall of Fame member Duke of Magenta broke his maiden in the 1877 Flash. *Courtesy of the National Museum of Racing.*

It was not run in 1896, when the track was closed; in 1911–12, when betting was made illegal in New York State; and in 1960. It was held at Belmont Park from 1943 through 1945, when Saratoga was closed because of World War II travel restrictions. After a hiatus from 1972 through 1980, it was held at Belmont in 1981 and 1982, and it returned to Belmont from 1999 through 2005, after which the race was terminated.

The best field to run in the Flash was the 1879 edition. The winner, Sensation, who never raced after his two-year-old season, was a perfect eight for eight, all stakes. The second-place horse, Grenada, finished second six times and placed third once in seven races against Sensation. As a three-year-old in 1880, he won the Potomac, Preakness, Belmont, Lorillard, Coney Island Derby and Travers. The 1880 three-year-old filly champion, Rosalie, was third.

The fourth-place horse, Luke Blackburn, was obviously slow to mature, as he was still a maiden after seven starts going into the Flash. After losing the Flash, he lost three more times before winning an overnight and the Ocean Stakes at Monmouth to close out a less-than-stellar season. In 1880 and 1881, he was almost unbeatable, compiling a record of twenty-four wins in twenty-five starts—in his only loss, he fell while in the lead—on his way to a well-deserved induction into the Hall of Fame.

Other notable fields in the Flash were 1882 (two-year-old and three-year-old champion George Kinney first and Hall of Fame filly Miss Woodford third), 1913 (Hall of Famer Old Rosebud first and future handicap star Stromboli second), 1918 (two-year-old champion male Billy Kelly first and 1919 Triple Crown winner and Hall of Fame inductee Sir Barton ninth) and 1938 (Hall of Fame inductees Eight Thirty first and Johnstown fourth).

Saratoga's Top Fifteen Fields

There have been plenty of great horses involved in major races at Saratoga Race Course over the years. Some showdowns lived up to and perhaps exceeded expectations. Others did not.

In his role as the historian at the National Museum of Racing and Hall of Fame, Allan Carter has spent a decade doing research on racing history. With this book in mind, he assigned himself the task of compiling a list of the best fifteen fields, in order of preference, to compete at Saratoga.

The main criteria used, and occasionally ignored, are that at least one horse in the race had to be a Hall of Fame inductee and at least two others had to either be in the Hall of Fame or been a divisional champion.

Since champions were not officially designated until 1936, he relied on two retrospective polls: the Historical Consensus published in *Blood-Horse* and a similar list that is found at Thoroughbred Heritage (www.tbheritage.com).

Most of the races selected took place more than sixty years ago, when the top horses had longer careers on the track and ran more often, when there were fewer big stakes to choose from and when owners and trainers were more willing to take on other standouts.

1. Wilson Stakes, August 5, 1946 (1 Mile)

Pavot (born 1942, Case Ace-Coquelicot), first, 126 pounds. Champion two-year-old male of 1944. Other stakes won that year included the Sussex Handicap (beating Gallorette and Stymie) and the Massachusetts Handicap (beating Gallorette).

Gallorette (born 1942, Challenger II-Gallette), second, 121 pounds. Champion 1946 handicap mare and Horse of the Year. Of her seventy-two career starts, fifty-five were against males, usually the best in their division. A 1955 poll of trainers named her the best filly/mare in American history. She was inducted into the Hall of Fame in 1962.

Polynesian (born 1942, Unbreakable-Black Polly), fourth, 117 pounds. Named champion sprinter in 1947. Stakes wins included the Toboggan, Roseben, Pageant, Scarsdale and Riggs. He is best known as the sire of Native Dancer.

Stymie (born 1941, Equestrian-Stop Watch), fifth, 120 pounds. Named champion older horse in 1945, this reformed claimer was the first Thoroughbred to win $900,000 in his career. His 1946 stakes wins were the Grey Lag Handicap, Whitney, Saratoga Cup (in a walkover) and the Edgemere, Manhattan, New York and Gallant Fox Handicaps. He was inducted into the Hall of Fame in 1975.

Pavot edging the Hall of Fame filly Gallorette in the 1946 Wilson. *Courtesy of the National Museum of Racing.*

Lucky Draw (born 1941, Jack High-Tatanne), seventh, 126 pounds. He ran against the best handicap horses of his generation, some of whom were in this race, and he managed to win the 1946 Butler (against Stymie and Gallorette, carrying a light 105 pounds), Monmouth Handicap (beating Stymie), Merchants' and Citizens' Handicap (beating Polynesian), Saratoga Handicap (beating Polynesian, Stymie and Pavot) and Narragansett Special (beating Pavot and Armed, that year's champion older male).

Larky Day (third), First Fiddle (sixth), King Dorsett (eighth), Bounding Home (ninth), The Doge (tenth) and Coincidence (eleventh) also ran.

2. Saratoga Handicap, July 31, 1916 (1¼ Miles)

Stromboli (born 1911, Fair Play-St. Priscilla), first, 121 pounds. He ran against the best handicap horses of his generation, especially Roamer. He was usually competitive against that foe and actually beat him in several races. His stakes wins included the 1914 Jerome and Manhattan and the 1915 Metropolitan and Suburban.

Friar Rock (born 1913, Rock Sand-Fairy Gold), third, 107 pounds. Champion three-year-old and Horse of the Year in 1916 after winning that year's Suburban Handicap, Belmont, Brooklyn Handicap and Saratoga Cup.

Stromboli was the winner of the 1916 Saratoga Handicap. *Courtesy of the National Museum of Racing.*

Short Grass (born 1908, Laverno-Outburst), fourth, 132 pounds. Co-champion handicap male in 1916 with Roamer. A prominent stakes winner in Europe, he came over to the United States in the fall of 1914 and won such stakes as the 1915 Empire City (defeating Roamer, Spur, Stromboli, Friar Rock and so on) and the 1916 Brookdale, Queens County, Bowie and Dixie Handicaps.

The Finn (born 1912, Ogden-Livonia), seventh,

123 pounds. Champion three-year-old male of 1915. His 1916 stakes wins included, in succession, the Champlain, Merchants' and Citizens' Chesterbrook and Havre de Grace Handicaps.

Regret (born 1912, Broomstick-Jersey Lightening), eighth and last, 123 pounds. Champion two-year-old filly of 1914 and champion three-year-old filly and Horse of the Year in 1915. Best known as the first filly to win the Kentucky Derby, her debacle in the 1916 Saratoga Handicap was the first loss of her career. She was inducted into the Hall of Fame in 1957.

Ed Crump (second), Chiclet (fifth) and Trial By Jury (sixth) also ran.

3. SARATOGA HANDICAP, JULY 30, 1928 (1¼ MILES)

Chance Shot (born 1924, Fair Play-Quelle Chance), first by 1 1/2, 122 pounds. His other stakes wins included the 1926 Saratoga Special, the 1927 Withers and Belmont and the 1928 Merchants' and Citizens' Handicap.

Chance Shot defeated some future Hall of Famers in the 1928 Saratoga Handicap. *Photo by Bert Clark Thayer. Courtesy of the National Museum of Racing.*

Black Maria (born 1923, Black Toney-Bird Loose), second, 115 pounds. Co-champion three-year-old filly with Edith Cavell in 1926 and champion older female in 1927 and 1928. Prominent among her stakes wins were the 1926 and 1927 Ladies' Handicap, the 1926 Kentucky Oaks, the 1926 and 1927 Aqueduct Handicap, the 1927 Metropolitan and Edgemere Handicaps and the 1928 Whitney.

Edith Cavell (born 1923, Man o' War-The Nurse), third, 106 pounds. Co-champion three-year-old filly with Black Maria in 1926. That year, she defeated Black Maria in the Coaching Club American Oaks and the Latonia Oaks and beat Crusader in the Pimlico Cup. She also won the 1927 Bowie Handicap and Pimlico Cup.

Sun Beau (born 1925, Sun Briar-Beautiful Lady), fourth, 109 pounds. Co-champion older male horse in 1929 with Diavolo and 1930 with Blue Larkspur, he won seventeen stakes between 1928 and 1931. He was inducted into the Hall of Fame in 1996.

Crusader (born 1923, Man o' War-Star Fancy), fifth, 127 pounds. Champion three-year-old male and Horse of the Year in 1926. Among his accomplishments were winning the Suburban Handicap two years in a row (1926 and 1927) and a sweep of the Suburban, Belmont and Jockey Club Gold Cup in the same year (1926). He was inducted into the Hall of Fame in 1995.

Dolan (sixth), Dangerous (seventh) and Barbara (eighth) also ran.

4. SARATOGA HANDICAP, AUGUST 1, 1917 (1¼ MILES)

Roamer (born 1911, Knight Errant-Rose Tree II), first, 122 pounds. Champion handicap male in 1915 and co-champion in 1916 with Short Grass. Perhaps his most famous race was at Saratoga in 1918 when he set a new world record for a mile while racing against the clock. He was inducted into the Hall of Fame in 1981.

Spur (born 1913, King James-Auntie Mum), second, 123 pounds. In 1916, he won eight races in twenty-one starts, including the Withers, Knickerbocker Handicap, Travers, Huron Handicap and Jerome Handicap. His stakes wins in 1917 included the Empire City Handicap (beating Borrow and Roamer), the Yonkers Handicap and the Monumental (beating Roamer).

Old Rosebud (born 1911, Uncle-Ivory Bells), fifth, 122 pounds. Champion two-year-old male in 1913 and champion older handicap horse and Horse of

Roamer prevailed against multi-stakes winner Spur in the 1917 Saratoga Handicap. *Courtesy of the National Museum of Racing.*

the Year in 1917. Among his stakes wins in 1917 were the Clark, Inaugural, Queens County, Carter and Delaware Handicaps. He was inducted into the Hall of Fame in 1968.

Campfire (born 1914, Olambala-Nightfall), sixth, 105 pounds. Champion two-year-old male of 1916 when he won the Hopeful, Futurity and Saratoga Special among other stakes. He went sour in 1917, losing his last three races by great margins, and was retired after this race.

Borrow (born 1908, Hamburg-Forget), seventh and last, 124 pounds. Co-champion older male in 1914 with Great Britain. His greatest win came in the 1917 Brooklyn Handicap when he beat three former Kentucky Derby winners—Regret, Old Rosebud and Omar Khayyam—as well as Roamer, Boots and Stromboli.

Ticket (third) and George Smith, the 1916 Kentucky Derby winner (fourth), also ran.

5. SARATOGA HANDICAP, JULY 31, 1905 (1¼ MILES)

Caughnawaga (born 1899, Clifford-La Tosca), first, 119 pounds. Hurricana Stud Farm stablemate of Molly Brant. In addition to this race, he also beat Beldame in the 1905 Saratoga Cup.

Beldame (born 1901, Octagon-Bella-Donna), third, 120 pounds. Champion three-year-old filly and Horse of the Year in 1904 and older female champion in 1905. She beat older males in the 1904 Carter, First Special, Second Special and Saratoga Cup, and in 1905, in addition to the Suburban Handicap, she won the Standard, also against males. She was inducted into the Hall of Fame in 1956.

Tanya (born 1902, Meddler-Handspun), fifth, 109 pounds. Co-champion two-year-old filly of 1904 and co-champion three-year-old filly of 1905 with her stablemate and future Hall of Fame inductee Artful. In 1904, she became the only filly to win the Spinaway and Hopeful at Saratoga, and in 1905, she won the Belmont Stakes.

Molly Brant (born 1900, Clifford-Ballyroe), sixth, 114 pounds. She was one of the most popular fillies to run at Saratoga. Although she was small, she

Caughnawaga beat three standout female runners in the 1905 Saratoga Handicap. *Courtesy of Sam Hildebrandt.*

won the 1903 Saranac and Hunter, the 1904 and 1905 Delaware Handicap and the 1904 Merchants' and Citizens' Handicap, all against males.

Ort Wells (born 1901, King Eric-Tea's Over), seventh, 126 pounds. Co-champion older male in 1905 with Delhi. He won such stakes as the 1904 Tidal and Lawrence Realization and the 1905 Brighton Mile.

Water Light (second), Wild Mint (fourth) and Alan-a-Dale (eighth) also ran.

6. Travers, August 22, 1987 (1¼ Miles)

Java Gold (born 1984, Key to the Mint-Javamina), first, 126 pounds. His Travers win was preceded by a win in the Whitney (beating Gulch, Broad Brush and Gone West) and was followed by a win in the Marlboro Cup and a second to Crème Fraiche as the 3-5 favorite in The Jockey Club Gold Cup.

Cryptoclearance (born 1984, Fappiano-Naval Orange), second, 126 pounds. Winner of the 1987 Florida Derby and Pegasus Handicap, as well

Java Gold handled the mud and a talented cast in the 1987 Travers. *Courtesy of NYRA/ Bob Coglianese.*

Owner Paul Mellon and Java Gold after the 1987 Travers. *Courtesy of NYRA/Bob Coglianese.*

as finishing second in the Flamingo and Belmont. He later won the 1986 and 1987 Hawthorne Gold Cup and the 1989 Donn and Widener Handicaps.

Polish Navy (born 1984, Danzig-Navsup) third, 126 pounds. A winner of the 1986 Champagne and Cowdin and 1987 Jim Dandy and Woodward (beating Gulch and Crème Fraiche).

Gulch (born 1984, Mr. Prospector-Jameela), fourth, 126 pounds. Named champion sprinter in 1988 after winning the Breeders' Cup Sprint. His 1987 wins included the Metropolitan Handicap (which he also won in 1988), Wood Memorial and Bay Shore.

Bet Twice (born 1984, Sportin' Life-Golden Dust), fifth, 126 pounds. He won two Grade 1 stakes at two and the Haskell Invitational Handicap, Belmont and Fountain of Youth in 1987.

Alysheba (born 1984, Alydar-Bel Sheba), sixth, 126 pounds. Named champion three-year-old male in 1987 and champion older male and Horse of the Year in 1988. Among his 1987 stakes victories were the Kentucky Derby, Preakness and Super Derby, as well as a second by a nose to Ferdinand in that year's Breeders' Cup Classic, which he won in 1988. He was inducted into the Hall of Fame in 1993.

Fortunate Moment (seventh), Temperate Sil (eighth) and Gorky (ninth) also ran.

7. New York Turf Writers Cup Handicap, August 14, 1980 (2⅜ Miles)

Zaccio (born 1976, Lorenzaccio-Delray Dancer), first, 157 pounds. Steeplechase Horse of the Year in 1980, 1981 and 1982. Among his stakes wins were two Colonial Cups (1981 and 1982) and two New York Turf Writers Cups (1980 and 1982). He was inducted into the Hall of Fame in 1990.

Running Comment (born 1974, Mongo-Craftyette), second, 142 pounds. His wins included the 1981 edition of this race, the 1980 and 1984 National Steeplechase Handicap and the 1982 International Gold Cup Steeplechase Handicap.

Steeplechase champion Zaccio on his way to victory in 1981 at Montpelier Station, Virginia. *Courtesy of the National Museum of Racing/Douglas Lees.*

Leaping Frog (born 1973, Tulpehocken-Admiration) third, 152 pounds. Stakes wins included the 1978 Lovely Night Steeplechase Handicap, the 1978 edition of this race and the 1980 Temple Gwathmey Steeplechase Handicap.

Martie's Anger (born 1975, Spring Double-Martie's Mad), fourth, 159 pounds. The 1979 Steeplechase Horse of the Year after winning that year's Colonial Cup, International Steeplechase Handicap and two other stakes. He also won the 1980 International Gold Cup Steeplechase Handicap.

Café Prince (born 1970, Crème Dela Crème-Blue Prince), sixth, eased, 161 pounds. Steeplechase Horse of the Year in 1977 and 1978. Among his stakes wins were the 1974 and 1979 Lovely Night Steeplechase Handicap and the 1975 and 1977 Colonial Cup Steeplechase Handicap. He was inducted into the Hall of Fame in 1985.

Leaping Frog, Martie's Anger and Café Prince were a Jonathan Sheppard entry.

Two Few Stripes (fifth) and Archange d'Or (seventh, left course) also ran.

8. Delaware Handicap, August 8, 1905 (1 Mile)

Molly Brant (see description in no. 5, the 1905 Saratoga Handicap), first, 113 pounds.

Beldame (see description in no. 5, the 1905 Saratoga Handicap), fifth, 122 pounds.

Roseben (born 1901, Ben Strome-Rose Leaf), sixth, 122 pounds. Of his fifty-two wins from 111 starts, he only won one race over 7½ furlongs. One of the greatest weight carriers of all time, he won fourteen races while carrying more than 140 pounds. He was inducted into the Hall of Fame in 1956.

Dolly Spanker (born 1901, Lady Gay-St. Gatia), second, 109 pounds. A winner of eight stakes in 1904, the gelding later beat Molly Brant in the Champlain.

Cairngorm (third), Monsieur Beauclaire (fourth) and Von Trump (seventh) also ran.

9. MERCHANTS' AND CITIZENS' HANDICAP, AUGUST 16, 1904 (1⅛ MILES)

Molly Brant (see description in no. 5, the 1905 Saratoga Handicap), first, 117 pounds.

Broomstick (born 1901, Ben Brush-Elf), second, 112 pounds. Winner of the 1904 Brighton Beach Handicap (beating Irish Lad, Waterboy and Ort Wells), Travers and Flying Handicap, he is considered one of the dominant sires of the first quarter of the twentieth century. He was inducted into the Hall of Fame in 1956.

Africander (born 1900, Star Ruby-Afric Queen), fourth, 123 pounds. Champion three-year-old male of 1903 after winning the Belmont, Suburban, Advance, Lawrence Realization, Saratoga Cup and Champlain. He also won the 1904 Brighton Cup.

Major Daingerfield (born 1899, Handspring-Mon Droit), sixth, 119 pounds. He competed against the best handicap horses of his generation,

Molly Brant defeated Beldame and Roseben in the 1905 Delaware Handicap. *Courtesy of Sam Hildebrandt.*

with limited success. Winner of the 1904 Parkway, Standard and Long Island Handicaps.

Reservation (third), Dainty (fifth), High Chancellor (seventh) and Lord of the Vale (eighth) also ran.

10. SARATOGA HANDICAP, AUGUST 2, 1920 (1¼ MILES)

Sir Barton (born 1916, Star Shoot-Lady Starling), first, 129 pounds. Champion three-year-old male and Horse of the Year in 1919 after becoming the first horse to win the Triple Crown, although it wasn't recognized as something special at the time. He also won the 1920 Merchants' and Citizens' Handicap. He was inducted into the Hall of Fame in 1957.

Exterminator (born 1915, McGee-Fair Empress), fourth, 126 pounds. Champion older male horse in 1920, 1921 (with Mad Hatter) and 1922 (with Grey Lag) and Horse of the Year in 1922. One of the greatest handicap horses in history, he won half of his one hundred starts, thirty-three of them stakes. He was inducted into the Hall of Fame in 1957.

Wildair (born 1917, Broomstick-Verdure) third, 115 pounds. Unfortunately born the same year as Man o' War, he nevertheless managed to win the 1920 Marathon Handicap (beating Sir Barton), the Metropolitan Handicap and the Empire City Derby.

The Porter (born 1915, Sweep-Ballet Girl), fourth, 124 pounds. He ran against such top handicap stars as Exterminator, Cudgel and Sir Barton. His

Triple Crown winner Sir Barton added to his legacy with a win over Exterminator in the 1920 Saratoga Handicap. *Courtesy of the Keeneland Library.*

most notable wins were in the 1919 Laurel Handicap, in which he defeated Billy Kelly and Sun Briar and the 1921 Annapolis Handicap, beating Exterminator while in receipt of fifteen pounds.

Mad Hatter (born 1916, Fair Play-Mad Cap), fifth and last, 118 pounds. Co-champion older male in 1921 with Exterminator, he won the 1921 and 1922 Metropolitan Handicap and the 1921 and 1922 Jockey Club Gold Cup.

11. Excelsior Sweepstakes, July 16, 1881 (1¼ Miles)

Checkmate (born 1875, Planet-Full Cry), first, 117 pounds. Co-champion older male horse of 1881. Slow to mature, Checkmate did not break his maiden until June 1879. He became a multiple stakes winner in 1880, and in 1881, he won seven of his eight races at Saratoga, including four stakes.

Thora (born 1878, Longfellow-Susan Ann), fourth, 107 pounds. Champion three-year-old filly of 1881 and champion older female of 1882. She won eight stakes in 1881, the most prominent being her ten-length win over Checkmate in the Pimlico Stakes. She also won five stakes in 1882, all over males.

Parole (born 1873, Leamington-Maiden), third, 117 pounds. Champion two-year-old male in 1875 and champion older male in 1877 (with Ten Broeck) and 1878 (Thoroughbred Heritage's Horse of the Year designations started with 1885). The gelding was immensely popular on both sides of the Atlantic. The 1881 Manhattan Handicap and Westchester Cup were the last two stakes wins of his career. Parole was inducted into the Hall of Fame in 1984.

Crickmore (born 1878, Catesby-Belle Meade), fourth, 102 pounds. Co-champion two-year-old male of 1880 with Hindoo. His 1881 stakes wins included the Dixie and Withers. He also ended Hindoo's eighteen-race win streak when he beat the obviously exhausted champion in the 1881 Brighton Beach Purse and beat him again in the September Handicap.

Bruno (fifth), Ripple (sixth), Uberto (seventh) and Oden (eighth) also ran.

12. Merchants' and Citizens' Handicap, August 23, 1919 (1 3/16 Miles)

Cudgel (born 1914, Broomstick-Eugenia Burch), first, 132 pounds. Champion older male in 1918 and co-champion in 1919 with Sun Briar. He came into prominence in 1918 with five stakes wins, the most important being the Brooklyn Handicap over Roamer. In 1919, in addition to the Merchants' and Citizens' Handicap, he beat Exterminator in the Havre de Grace Handicap.

Exterminator (see description in no. 10, the 1920 Saratoga Handicap), third, 126 pounds.

Sun Briar (born 1915, Sundridge-Sweet Briar), fourth, 132 pounds. Champion two-year-old male of 1917 and, inexplicably, co-champion older male in 1919. Although he won some stakes after 1917, he never reached the quality of his freshman year.

Star Master (second) and Polka Dot (fifth) also ran.

13. Windsor Hotel, August 14, 1880 (5 Furlongs)

Crickmore (see description in no. 11, the 1881 Excelsior), first, 107 pounds.

Hindoo (born 1878, Virgil-Flonnie), third, 110 pounds. Co-champion two-year-old male in 1880 with Crickmore, champion three-year-old male of 1881 and champion older male of 1882. He is best known for winning eighteen races from May 12 through September 1, 1881. He was inducted into the Hall of Fame in 1955.

Thora (see description in no. 11, the 1881 Excelsior), fourth, 107 pounds.

Bonnie Lizzie (second), Calycanthus (fifth), Little Nell (sixth), Alfambra (seventh) and Bride Cake (eighth) also ran.

14. Flash, July 22, 1879 (4 Furlongs)

Sensation (born 1877 Leamington-Susan Beane), first, 110 pounds. Champion two-year-old male of 1879, winning all eight of his starts, all of them stakes. He never raced again.

Grenada (born 1877, King Alfonso-Mattie Gross), second, 110 pounds. One of the unluckiest horses in history, he lost six times to Sensation as a two-year-old, and the next year, he had to contend with the brilliant Luke Blackburn. He still managed to win the 1879 Windsor Hotel and the 1880 Belmont, Lorillard, Long Island Derby, Travers and Jerome.

Rosalie (born 1877, Leamington-La Rose), third, 107 pounds. Champion two-year-old filly in 1879 despite winning only one stake, beating Grenada (seventh) in the Hopeful.

Luke Blackburn (born 1877, Bonnie Scotland-Nevada), fourth, 110 pounds. Champion three-year-old male in 1880. He was slow to mature, losing his first eleven starts as a two-year-old before winning his last two starts of the year. As a three-year-old, he lost his first start, then won six in a row before falling while in the lead at Gravesend. He then won his last fourteen races, beating some of the best horses in the country, often by wide margins. He won his first race in 1881 before his streak was stopped. He was inducted into the Hall of Fame in 1956.

Minos (fifth), Ferncliffe (sixth), Observanda (seventh) and Flibbertgibbet (eighth) also ran.

15. TRAVERS, AUGUST 17, 1918 (1¼ MILES)

Sun Briar (see description in no. 12, the 1919 Merchants' and Citizens' Handicap), first, 120 pounds.

Johren (born 1915, Spearmint-Mineola), second, 126 pounds. Champion older male and Horse of the Year in 1918. He didn't start racing until 1918, and he lost his first nine races. However, he soon made his mark by winning the Suburban, Belmont and Latonia Derby, and he ended his one-year career by winning, in succession, the Huron, Saratoga Cup and Lawrence Realization.

War Cloud (born 1915, Polymelus-Dreamy) third, 126 pounds. War Cloud won the first division of the 1918 Preakness, beating Johren and the rest, and he beat Johren again when he won the Dwyer. He won three other stakes that year.

Exterminator (see description in no. 10, the 1920 Saratoga Handicap), fourth, 123 pounds.

The 1918 Travers was the second time in American Thoroughbred history that three horses that won a Triple Crown race the same year met in

Willis Sharpe Kilmer's Sun Briar won the 1918 Travers, defeating the winners of the Triple Crown races. *Courtesy of the Keeneland Library.*

a later race (Exterminator, 1918 Kentucky Derby; War Cloud, first division of the 1918 Preakness; and Johren, 1918 Belmont).

Common Errors About Saratoga Racing

1. The Oklahoma training track was not the site where the first season was held.

Eight races over four days in August 1863 were contested on the trotting track at what is now known as Horse Haven. Oklahoma, which is adjacent to Horse Haven north of Union Avenue, was developed forty years after John Morrissey staged the first Thoroughbred meeting in Saratoga Springs. William C. Whitney purchased 102 acres in August 1902 that became the site of the Oklahoma facility in 1904.[34]

2. Though it is the oldest and now the best-known Saratoga race, the Travers spent decades in the shadow cast by the Hopeful and the Saratoga Cup. For many years, those two races were held on the final day of the meet and had more prestige and larger purses.

The Hopeful had so much value because of the added money that came from nominations to the race by the breeders and owners of young horses, the "hopefuls" in their stables. In fact, the winner's share of the Travers did not surpass the Hopeful until 1972. The Hopeful debuted in 1903 with a purse of $25,000, while the Travers carried a purse of $10,000 that summer. Twenty-five years later, the 1928 Hopeful had a value to the winner of $54,100, while the winner of the Travers collected $30,550. In 1972, Key to the Mint earned $66,600 for winning the Travers, while Secretariat's win in the Hopeful was worth $51,930 to Meadow Farm.

3. Saratoga was known as the nickname "Graveyard of Favorites" long before someone decided to amend it to "Graveyard of Champions" while describing how many outstanding horses went down to defeat at the old track on Union Avenue.

The online index of the *New York Times*, which has reported on Saratoga racing since the beginning, shows the first use of the expression "Graveyard of Favorites" to describe a Saratoga race in 1934 when Kievex upset Bazaar in the Saranac. The first use of "Graveyard of Champions" in the *Times* regarding Saratoga came on August 2, 1973, describing a loss the previous day by champ Riva Ridge. The story contained a description of the five thousand people who turned out to see a morning workout by Riva Ridge's stablemate Secretariat, who failed at the graveyard the next summer.

4. The 1982 Travers, which featured the three winners of the Triple Crown series, was not the first time the winners of the individual races met in the Travers. It was the second meeting of three winners in the Travers—the first was in 1918—and the fourth time overall.

Long shot Runaway Groom prevailed in 1982 over Kentucky Derby winner Gato Del Sol, Preakness winner Aloma's Ruler and Belmont Stakes winner Conquistador Cielo. In the 1918 Travers, held on August 17, Sun Briar finished first. The runner-up was Belmont winner Johren, while War Cloud, winner of the first division of the Preakness, was third. Fourth and last was Sun Briar's stablemate, Exterminator, who had won the Derby earlier in the year. The other times that separate winners of the Triple Crown races met were the 1875 Jerome Stakes and the 1929 Classic at Arlington Park. In the Jerome, the first Derby winner, Aristides, defeated Belmont winner Calvin and Preakness winner Tom Ochiltree. Belmont winner Blue Larkspur won the Classic at Arlington Park over Derby hero Clyde Van Dusen and Preakness winner Dr. Freeland.

5. The meaning of the word "upset" did not change to mean an unexpected outcome when Upset defeated Man o' War in the 1919 Sanford Memorial.

A review of older dictionaries shows that the usage was in place before Man o' War suffered the only loss of his career. A few weeks before the Sanford was held, the *New York Times* ran the headline, "Many Upsets in Golf Play: Favorites Put Out of the Running on New London Links."[35]

6. August Belmont's private training center, Surcingle, along Nelson Avenue south of the track, was named Clare Court in 1940 for Thomas Clare, not for Clare and his wife, Anne, who succeeded him as the track superintendent.[36]

Man o' War's loss in 1919 was a shocker but not a word-changer. *Courtesy of the Keeneland Library.*

Within a few months after Thomas Clare's sudden death in Florida at the age of sixty-three, the area was referred to as Clare Court in the *Saratogian.*[37]

7. The prominent Whitney Invitational Handicap was established in 1928 as a tribute to the late Payne Whitney rather than as a race to honor the Whitney family's contributions to Saratoga racing.

Payne Whitney, a son of William C. Whitney, died at the age of fifty-one in May 1927. Several newspapers, including the *Saratogian*, carried stories saying that the race was a memorial to Payne Whitney.[38] Although he was a member of The Jockey Club and had been involved in breeding before his death, Payne Whitney was not as deeply committed to racing as his wife, Helen Hay Whitney, who operated Greentree Stable, or brother, Harry Payne Whitney.

Hopeful and Spinaway Winner Tanya

After the death of William C. Whitney on February 2, 1904, most of his horses were leased to Herman B. Duryea for the 1904 racing season. In that group was a pair of talented two-year-old fillies, one by British import Meddler out of Handspun by Hanover named Tanya and the other a future Hall of Fame inductee named Artful. Both were trained by future Hall of Famer John W. Rogers.

Tanya won the first two starts of her career by going wire-to-wire in two-year-old purse races, setting a new world record for 4½ furlongs. In her third race, the National Stallion Stakes at Morris Park, she won by a head as the favorite over Belle Strome and Blandy—the latter of whom she had beaten easily in her previous race—and seven others. It was not only her first stakes win but also, as the *New York Times* pointed out, the first time she carried scale weight—119 pounds, as opposed to 122 pounds for colts.[39]

Tanya's reputation preceded her when she moved upstate to race in the Spinaway Stakes for two-year-old fillies at Saratoga. The *New York Times* noted that she was the granddaughter of the filly for whom the race was named, Spinaway being the dam of Handspun.[40] Her grandmother, who was sired by Leamington out of Megara, was the 1880 two-year-old filly champion after winning the Juvenile, Foam, Surf, Hopeful (at Monmouth Park), July and Chestnut Hill Stakes. Since Duryea also had Iota and Heart's Desire entered with Tanya in the six-horse field, the bookies limited the betting to place only. Tanya won easily, galloping out to win by two lengths.

Tanya completed the Hopeful-Spinaway double in 1904. *Courtesy of the National Museum of Racing.*

The next race on Tanya's horizon was the second running of Saratoga's Hopeful for two-year-olds of either sex. Running with Rose of Dawn and Heart's Desire, Tanya, who was the high weight of 127 pounds despite her sex, won easily by one and a half lengths. Finishing ninth was her personal punching bag, Blandy.

Not shy of using overstatement, the *New York Times* enthused that "her race to-day was the most remarkable run by a filly in the memory of turfmen, and her success left not the least room for question that Tanya ranks with the best of her age and sex that the American turf has ever produced."[41]

A little more restrained was the correspondent for the *New York Sunday Telegraph*: "Her performance is easily sufficient license for disputing with [Brighton Junior, Flash and Saratoga Special winner Sysonby] the right to the juvenile premiership of the turf."[42] Thus Tanya became the only filly to complete the Spinaway/Hopeful exacta at Saratoga. Bee Mac accomplished the same feat in 1943 at Belmont when Saratoga was closed due to World War II travel restrictions.

The *New York Times* encomium would be proved premature. Her next, and last, race for 1904 was the prestigious Futurity at Sheepshead Bay. Facing Tanya were two other undefeated two-year-olds, Sysonby and the filly Tradition, as well as the multi-stakes winner Oiseau. Although there were several subplots in the race, briefly the winner was Tanya's entrymate Artful, followed by Tradition, Sysonby and, in fourth, eight lengths from the winner, Tanya.

Artful was a maiden and earned the first of six consecutive victories. She had finished a well-held second in her first two starts because entrymates had been declared—a practice at the time—as the horse expected to win. Sysonby suffered the only loss of his Hall of Fame career in the Futurity. Supposedly, he was drugged by his groom, but that has never been substantiated. Tanya and Artful were named co-champion two-year-old fillies for 1904.

In the fall of 1904, Duryea's horse stock was sold at auction, and Tanya and Artful were moved to the stable of Harry Payne Whitney, who proved to be a more than worthy successor to his father as a horse owner. Tanya began her 1905 season with a third in a three-year-old allowance race at the newly built Belmont Park. Nine days later, on May 24, she became only the second filly to win the Belmont Stakes, against a field weakened by the absence of Sysonby and Artful. Finishing second was, of course, Blandy.

On June 3, Tanya faced Sysonby for the second time in the Lawrence Realization and, while finishing second, was not a factor. The omnipresent Blandy finished fourth. Tanya ended her 1905 season by finishing fifth in the Saratoga Handicap, which included such stars as Caughnawaga (first), Beldame (third) and Molly Brant (sixth).

Tanya did not race in 1906 and ended her career in 1907 by finishing second in a three-years-and-up handicap and last in a filly and mare handicap at Belmont Park.

As a broodmare, Tanya was a failure, unable to produce anything of note despite several dates with leading sire Broomstick. She was shipped to France in 1912, returning to the United States in 1919. She died in 1929.

Surprising Winners

Upset, Jim Dandy and Onion

Upset
(1917, Whisk Broom II-Pankhurst, by Voter)

On August 13, 1919, Upset handed Man o' War the only defeat of his career in the Sanford Memorial. Nearly a century later, it remains one of the most famous races in the history of the American turf.

A Harry Payne Whitney homebred trained by Hall of Famer James Rowe Sr., Upset spent his racing career in regal surroundings. His owner and breeder led the nation's owners in money earned in 1905, 1913, 1920, 1924, 1926, 1927 and 1929. Whitney also led the breeders in money earned in 1924—such statistics were not kept until 1923—and 1926 through 1930. Even after his death in 1930, his estate continued to lead in 1931 and 1932, and he and his son, C.V. Whitney, led in 1933, 1934 and 1938.

Among Whitney's horses were future Hall of Fame inductees Regret, Equipoise, Whisk Broom II and Artful, as well as such champions as Burgomaster, Johren, Whiskery and Victorian. Upset's sire, Whisk Broom II, raced in England from 1909 through 1912. He returned home in 1913 in time to become the first horse to sweep the Brooklyn, Suburban and Metropolitan before being retired due to an injury. Whisk Broom II was just as successful in the breeding shed, siring such standouts as Whiskaway, Victorian, Upset, John P. Grier, Diavolo and Whiskery.

The flaw in Upset's breeding was his dam, Pankhurst. Bred by Harry Payne Whitney, she was by Voter out of the Domino mare Runaway Girl.

Upset earned his place in racing history with his win over Man o' War in the 1919 Sanford Memorial. *Courtesy of the Keeneland Library/C.C. Cook.*

She had a short and undistinguished racing career, winning two of three races in 1912. Her breeding career wasn't very productive either. Of her eleven foals, Upset was the only one who had an even remotely successful career. Only two of Upset's four full siblings made it to the track, and only one, Dartmoor, broke his maiden.

Although Dartmoor had a total of five wins in thirty-eight starts, most of those wins came in claiming races after he left the Whitney ranks. His lone shining moment came in his first race on August 18, 1920, at Saratoga, when he won by a neck over another first-time starter, a 50-1 shot named Grey Lag, who would eventually be inducted into the Hall of Fame.

Upset might have been the second-best colt of the 1917 crop. There's no debate about who topped the list: Man o' War. All the other top-level horses were unlucky to be foaled the same year. Upset won two of eight starts in 1919, his maiden win and his victory over Man o' War in the Sanford Memorial. Four of his six losses that year were to Man o' War in the United States Hotel, Grand Union Hotel, Hopeful and Futurity.

In his sophomore year, Upset won two of six starts, and half of those losses came against Man o' War in the Preakness and Travers. His two wins were in the Havre de Grace Consolation Handicap and the Latonia Derby. He also finished second by a neck to Paul Jones in the Kentucky Derby and fourth to that same rival in the Suburban Handicap, with Exterminator finishing third.

Upset ended his career in 1921 with one win and one place from three starts. He finished second by a nose to Ginger in the Clark Handicap while

Upset with Willie Knapp up. *Courtesy of the Keeneland Library/C.C. Cook.*

giving that rival a ten-pound weight advantage. A week later, he finished sixth in the Kentucky Handicap as the 6-5 favorite and high weight with 124 pounds. His last race was a win in the Hillside Handicap at Belmont as the high weight with 121 pounds to his two opponents' 97 and 95.

Upset had a career record of five wins from seventeen starts and earnings of $37,504.

In 1922, Upset transitioned to stud duty. For the most part, Whitney and his son, C.V., loaned Upset to various farms in Kentucky. He did fairly well as a stallion, finishing second in 1928 and seventh in 1929 in the "Leading American Sires" section of the *American Racing Manual*. Among his best get in that time period were multi-stakes winners Misstep, a 1925 foal out of St. Theresa, and Windy City, born in 1926, out of Allivan. Upset died, unheralded, on March 21, 1941.

JIM DANDY
(1927, JIM GAFFNEY-THUNDERBIRD, BY STAR SHOOT)

With one improbable victory on August 11, 1930, over a sloppy track in the Travers, Jim Dandy made a name for himself that lives on. At odds of 100-1, he defeated that year's Triple Crown winner Gallant Fox, who was among the early selections when the Hall of Fame was established in the 1950s.

Jim Dandy's accomplishment was recognized in 1964 by the New York Racing Association, which named a prep race at Saratoga for the Travers in this honor.

Like Upset, Jim Dandy had a genealogy that was more noteworthy on his sire's side. A 1905 foal by the Irish import Golden Garter out of Miss Maxim, the California-bred Jim Gaffney lost his first five starts in 1907. However, two of those losses were at Saratoga to future Hall of Fame inductees Fair Play and Colin. He finished second to Fair Play in the Flash and was the runner-up to the undefeated Colin in the Grand Union Hotel.

On August 17, he broke his maiden in impressive style by winning the Hopeful, with Fair Play finishing second while conceding 5 pounds to the winner. He followed his Hopeful victory with a win in Saratoga's Albany Handicap and ended his successful campaign at the Spa by finishing second in the United States Hotel to Restigouche, who carried 109 pounds to Gaffney's 127. Finishing third was Fair Play under 125 pounds.

Jim Gaffney returned to Sheepshead Bay to race in the rich and prestigious Futurity, where he finished sixth to Colin, with Fair Play checking in fourth. He ran five more times downstate, with one win, two seconds and a third. Included in this skein was a fourth in the Nursery to Dorant, to whom he was conceding 32 pounds. His old rival Fair Play finished third under 122 pounds.

At season's end, Jim Gaffney had three wins, five seconds and one third from fourteen starts. Colin led all horses in earnings with $133,097, and Jim Gaffney's $25,445 placed him third among two-year-olds, behind Stamina but ahead of Fair Play, who earned $16,735.

The rest of Jim Gaffney's career didn't come close to fulfilling the promise he showed in 1907, possibly because of an injury. He only ran once in 1908, finishing out of the money in an allowance race at Oakland, where he spent the rest of his racing days. He enjoyed some success in California, although the competition was vastly inferior to what he met when he was racing against Fair Play and Colin.

Jim Gaffney retired after the 1911 to become a stallion. His breeding career was like his racing career: good but not great. Although he often appeared on the *American Racing Manual*'s "Twenty Leading American Sires" list, none of his get could match those of the perennial leaders Broomstick (Whisk Broom II, Regret and Cudgel), his old opponent Fair Play (Man o' War, Display and Mad Hatter) or English import Star Shoot (Sir Barton and Grey Lag).

The dam of Jim Dandy, Thunderbird, was a 1917 foal by Star Shoot out of Grace G. She did not have much success either as a racehorse or as a broodmare. In a four-year racing career, which lasted from 1919 through 1922, she had five wins, seven places and five shows from sixty-two starts, earning a grand total of $2,828. Not surprisingly, most of her career was spent in claiming races.

As a broodmare, she had seven foals, and besides Jim Dandy, the only ones to have had extensive racing careers were Ormonbird and Vimont, both sired by Ormont. The former, a 1925 foal, raced from 1928 through 1932 with ten wins in 89 starts and had career earnings of $13,752. Vimont, born a year later, raced from 1928 through 1933 with sixteen wins from 147 starts and earned $16,348. The best that one can say about Thunderbird is that her foals were durable.

After finishing fifth in his first career start on May 4, 1929, at the old Lexington track, Jim Dandy broke his maiden one week later on a sloppy track on Derby Day at Churchill Downs at odds of 19-1. Watching the race that day was trainer John B. McKee, who was looking for a horse for his owner, twenty-one-year-old oil heir Chaffee Earl. Suitably impressed, McKee was happy to pay Jim Dandy's owner and breeder, W.S. Dudley, the $25,000 asking price.

Under McKee's care, Jim Dandy finished second in an allowance race and fourth in the Bashford Manor at Churchill Downs, then was given a break of

Unheralded Jim Dandy won the 1930 Travers at odds of 100-1. *Courtesy of the Keeneland Library.*

almost three months and was shipped to Saratoga. He made an immediate impression when he won the Grand Union Hotel Stakes at odds of 50-1 on, as usual, a sloppy track. The rest of his season was not as successful, as he finished twelfth and last in the Hopeful at Saratoga and was off the board in three starts at Laurel.

The beginning of his 1930 campaign was as dismal as his post–Grand Union Hotel season. Jim Dandy started the year at Agua Caliente in Tijuana, Mexico, which was not known as a popular site to prep future three-year-old champions. He finished off the board in his first eight starts at that track before finishing third on March 21 in a handicap event. Undeterred, McKee gave Jim Dandy a rest in California before shipping him to Saratoga for the Burnt Hills Handicap. Showing that his performances in Mexico were not flukes, he finished eighth out of nine horses. The only horse he beat threw his jockey.

Although not an ideal prep for a meeting with a Triple Crown winner, Jim Dandy was scratched from an earlier allowance race on the Travers card to go in the feature. He shocked a packed house that had braved the rotten weather to see the showdown between Gallant Fox and Whichone, the two-year-old champion of 1929, by splashing to an eight-length victory.

The rest of his sophomore season was rather dismal and a portent of his future. In his nine remaining starts, he finished on the board only once, a third in the Cambridge Handicap at Laurel. However, he lost to some champion horses, such as Questionnaire, Petee-Wrack, future Hall of Famer Sun Beau, and 1929 Preakness winner Dr. Freedland.

The Travers was his only win in twenty starts that year and was Gallant Fox's only loss in ten starts.

Jim Dandy's 1931 season was, at best, unspectacular. He began with four losses at Saratoga, although he did manage to finish third in a handicap race and the Merchants' and Citizens' Handicap. He also raced at Hawthorne and Tanforan with little success. While he won his only race of the year in a claiming event at Tanforan, perhaps the highlight of his season was a second in the Mid-West Handicap at Hawthorne. Finishing in his wake in sixth, two and a half lengths from the winner, was Sun Beau, who was spotting the Travers winner twenty pounds.

The rest of Jim Dandy's career was mainly losing efforts in minor purse events at third-rate tracks. Chaffee Earl finally got discouraged and gave his horse to McKee, which was an excellent move since the trainer had a great deal of affection for the horse despite his losing efforts. Jim Dandy raced until 1939, his last win coming on May 30, 1933, in the Memorial Day

Handicap at Riverside Park, Kansas City, Missouri. The odds were, as usual, high at 17-1, and the purse was $1,000. His lifetime record was seven wins, six seconds and eight thirds from 141 starts.

Jim Dandy's life after his retirement was apparently a happy one. According to Debra Ginsburg, whose article is the best source for Jim Dandy's post-Travers career, McKee died shortly after his horse's retirement. However, before his death, he arranged for Jim Dandy to be taken by L.G. Otto, who owned a racing academy in Glendale, California. He became an excellent dressage horse, and his ability to jump over high fences led Ms. Ginsburg to speculate that he would have had more success as a steeplechase horse.[43] Although there are no reports of his death, he apparently lived his last days as a horse of leisure in Southern California.

Onion
(1969, Third Martini-With a Flair, by Beau Gar)

Two years before his election to the Hall of Fame, trainer H. Allen Jerkens added to his fine reputation on August 4, 1973, with Onion's shocking victory over Secretariat, the 1-10 favorite in the Grade 2 Whitney. The fact that the Triple Crown winner was suffering from a virus, an illness that would keep him out of the Travers two weeks later, did nothing to dim Onion's achievement.

Onion's dam, With a Flair, a 1964 foal by Beau Gar out of Mopkins, had a brief but relatively successful career as a racehorse. As a two-year-old, she won five of her ten races but was off the board in four stakes, with earnings of $31,586. In 1967, she lost her only race, finishing twelfth and last in Hialeah's Florida Breeders' Handicap before being retired.

Although she was mated with such noted sires as Ribot, Raise a Native and Dr. Fager, Onion was With a Flair's most successful foal. His full brother, Three Onions, born a year before Onion, toiled as a claimer for most of his eight-year career. Vincent, by Ribot, was a 1972 foal that eventually dropped into the claiming ranks after failing in turf events, which were obviously chosen because of his sire. Although he had a thoroughly undistinguished career, Vincent became With a Flair's only other foal to win a stakes race when as a seven-year-old he captured the $3,600 Peter Lane Marathon at Regina, Saskatchewan.

One foal out of With a Flair who might have had a good career was Subtle Slip, by Raise a Native. The filly, although a maiden in her only year

Onion drives through the stretch to best Secretariat in the 1973 Whitney. *Courtesy of NYRA/ Bob Coglianese.*

of racing, was never off the board in five starts. She was the favorite in four of those starts and was disqualified from what would have been her only win. All of With a Flair's other foals either had undistinguished careers or never raced.

Third Martini, a 1959 foal by Hasty Road out of The Golden Girl, had a seven-year career as a durable and capable racehorse. Bred and originally owned by Paul Mellon's Rokeby Stable, he won four of nine starts for Rokeby from 1961 through July 13, 1963, when he was sold to Hobeau Farm. He raced for that stable through the 1967 season, winning the 1964 Spy Song Handicap at Garden State, Longport Handicap at Monmouth, Knickerbocker and Queens County Handicaps at Aqueduct and the 1967 Palm Beach at Hialeah. He retired with a career total of twenty-three wins from fifty-seven starts and earnings of $231,304.

As a sire, Third Martini was fairly successful. Although he never made *Daily Racing Form*'s annual list of top thirty sires, he had some notable foals besides Onion. Toonerville, out of Powerful Katrinka, won the Bougainvillea, W.L. McKnight and Florida Turf Cup with earnings of $257,892. Another,

Three Martinis, out of Three Fingers, won the Great American and Saratoga Special, with earnings of $195,501.

Onion was a gelded Hobeau Farm homebred who began his career in 1972 with a modest record of two wins in eight starts when he inaugurated what was to be a successful career at Saratoga by defeating the 1971 Kentucky Derby and Preakness winner Canonero II by six lengths in an August 12 allowance race. Ten days later, he won another allowance race at the Spa, beating, among others, the 1970 Travers winner Loud. He ended his 1972 season on September 7 with a sixth in an allowance race at Belmont as the even-money favorite, giving him a record of four wins, three seconds and one third from eleven starts with earnings of $36,320.

He began his 1973 season much like 1972, as he won or was competitive in minor or overnight stakes races. He lost to such horses as King's Bishop and Explodent and managed to beat Loud two more times. The stage was now set for his invasion of Saratoga. His upstate campaign began auspiciously on July 31, four days before his historic race with Secretariat, when he won the Dike Purse by eight lengths, setting a new but short-lived track record of 1:15 1/5 for 6½ furlongs. Finishing second in that race was Spanish Riddle, who one year earlier had set a new track record of 1:08 for 6 furlongs, a record that still stands.

After his stunning win in the Whitney, the newly renowned Onion finished seventh in the Governor Stakes at Belmont and fourth in the inaugural Marlboro Cup at Belmont. The Marlboro may have been his best race of his career. The three horses who finished ahead of him—Secretariat, Riva Ridge and Cougar II—have since been enshrined in the Hall of Fame. The three he beat were Kennedy Road, a multiple stakes–winning Canadian star who that year had won the Grade 1 Hollywood Gold Cup and San Antonio, as well as other graded stakes; Annihilate 'Em, the winner of that year's Grade 1 Travers, albeit by default, due to the scratch of Secretariat, who was ill; and Key to the Mint, the previous year's champion three-year-old male and the 1973 winner of the Grade 1 Suburban Handicap and Grade 2 Excelsior.

Onion finished his four-year-old season by winning two of three purse events at Aqueduct in December, giving him a record of six wins, six places and one show from sixteen starts with earnings of $130,337.

Due to a bowed tendon, Onion had to bypass the 1974 campaign, but he returned to run a somewhat abbreviated six-year-old season. From February 15 through May 26, he ran twelve times, compiling a record of five wins, two places and two shows. Although all his wins came in overnight purse events, he also competed in several graded events. The first was the Westchester Handicap on March 29, in which he finished third to his stablemate Step Nicely. On May 17, he finished seventh in the Carter Handicap to the last of the great weight carriers and future Hall of Famer Forego.

His last race of the year was on May 26 in the prestigious Metropolitan Handicap, popularly known as the Met Mile. Onion was ahead at the half but dropped back sharply and finished eighth and last. Finishing ahead of him were such stalwarts as the winner Gold and Myrrh, Stop the Music, Forego (who was carrying 136 pounds) and his stablemate Group Plan, who later that year won The Jockey Club Gold Cup. Since he was out for the rest of the year and all of 1976, it is possible that he suffered an injury in the Met Mile. Unfortunately, the reason for that long layoff is not known.

Onion came back in 1977, but he was a mere shadow of his former self. He ran fourteen times, all but one of them claiming events, and he won twice. He returned once to his favorite track, but he spoiled his perfect four-for-four record by finishing seventh in a $35,000 claiming race.

Onion was retired after the 1977 season and lived the peaceful life of a pensioner at Hobeau Farm in Ocala, Florida, where he died on October 24, 1995, at the age of twenty-six.

An Ode to the Popular Molly Brant

I n the early years of the twentieth century, the gutty Molly Brant captured the hearts of Saratoga racing fans.

A diminutive filly by Clifford out of the British import Ballynoe by Fullerton, she was a 1900 foal bred and owned by the Sanford family's Hurricana Stud Farm in nearby Amsterdam. The Sanfords occasionally named their horses after Native Americans indigenous to the Mohawk Valley, such as Caughnawaga, Chuctununda and Mohawk II. Molly Brant was named after an eighteenth-century Mohawk woman who was for many years a consort of Sir William Johnson. After his death in 1774, Molly Brant and her six children by Johnson returned to the Mohawk Valley, but because of her British connection, she made a permanent move to British Canada after the beginning of the Revolutionary War.

Molly Brant (the horse) was aptly described by turf historian Walter Vosburgh: "She had the Bonnie Scotland [the sire of Clifford's sire, Bramble] toughness joined to that of the unbeaten Barcaldine [the Irish-bred sire of Ballynoe's dam, Caledonia], and became such a favorite from her sterling honesty and courage the sturdy yeomen of the Mohawk Valley never failed to come in hundreds to see her race and never failed to cheer her to the echo."[44]

Molly Brant's career started inauspiciously in 1902 when she finished eighth and thirteenth, by disqualification, in her first two races at Saratoga. Like all Sanford horses, her racing season did not start until after Saratoga opened. A hint of her future ability was shown in her third race, the Adirondack Handicap for two-year-olds, when she beat fourteen other horses to break

The Sanford family's Molly Brant with foal. *Courtesy of Sam Hildebrandt.*

her maiden at 10-1. Finishing last in that race was Africander, who went on to be the 1903 champion three-year-old male and was a frequent opponent of Molly Brant's.

Following that maiden win, she finished her freshman campaign with a sixth in a two-year-old handicap at Saratoga while carrying high weight of 122 pounds, and she also won one of three races downstate. One of her losses, a second by a head in Gravesend's Willow Stakes to Astarita, was another portent of things to come. Astarita had won two previous stakes, but nevertheless, she enjoyed a 7-pound weight advantage over Molly Brant.

Although she only raced twice at Saratoga as a three-year-old, both races were significant. In her seasonal debut, she finished second by a head to the outstanding four-year-old Hermis, who was the previous year's three-year-old male champion and Horse of the Year and would repeat as champion older male horse and Horse of the Year in 1903. Because of her age and sex, Molly Brant was given a twenty-five-pound weight advantage over her older opponent.

In her second and last race at Saratoga in 1903, she won the Saranac Handicap for three-year-olds. The 9-5 favorite in the race was Shorthose, who was coming off a second to Injunction in Saratoga's Kenner Stakes.

Finishing fourth was the 4-1 second choice, Africander, who was carrying high weight of 127 pounds to Molly Brant's 100.

In her next race, the Ocean at Sheepshead Bay at a distance of one mile, once again she was second to Hermis by a head, while enjoying a twenty-two-pound weight advantage. With the exception of a win in the Hunter Handicap at Morris Park, the remainder of her fall campaign was the worst stretch of her career. She lost five races, the last two as the favorite at Brighton Beach.

Molly Brant rebounded from her relatively dismal campaign downstate by starting the 1904 season winning her first four starts at Saratoga. After she opened the year with a win in a one-mile handicap, she swept the Delaware, Merchants' and Citizens' and Champlain Handicaps. The opening handicap race was notable because the place horse, Reliable, was one of the best sprinters in the country and the 7-5 favorite in the race. Her win in the Merchants' and Citizens' Handicap was the most important victory of her career. The *New York Times* described the race as "one of the best fields of the meeting."[45] Among her opponents were future Hall of Fame inductee Broomstick, a three-year-old that six weeks earlier had set a new world record for $1\frac{1}{4}$ miles in the Brighton Handicap and had just won the Travers; Dainty, a California invader who had previously won the Thistle at Sheepshead Bay and the Islip Handicap at Brighton Beach and would later win the Occidental and Oriental handicaps; Major Daingerfield, who ran against the top handicap horses in the country and occasionally won; and Lord of the Vale, who had earlier won the Seashore Handicap at Brighton Beach and the Saratoga Handicap.

Molly Brant's 1904 fall campaign at the New York metropolitan tracks consisted of two races, a second to Broomstick in an allowance race at Sheepshead Bay and a second to Carbuncle, to whom she was giving twenty-one pounds, in a handicap at Morris Park.

She began her 1905 (and final) season at Saratoga on July 31 by finishing sixth to her stablemate, Caughnawaga, in the Saratoga Handicap. Also in that race were future Hall of Fame filly Beldame, who was third, and that year's champion older male horse, Ort Wells, who was seventh. Eight days later, Molly won her second straight Delaware, defeating Beldame, who finished fifth. She ended her career at Saratoga in the Champlain Handicap with a second by a head as the 7-10 favorite to the four-year-old gelding Dolly Spanker, to whom she was conceding thirteen pounds. That same opponent finished second to Molly Brant in the previous Delaware Handicap while enjoying a five-pound pull in the weights.

By this point, Molly Brant's popularity with the bettors was at a zenith, as described by the *New York Times*: "The people from Amsterdam, the home of Molly Brant, held her in great respect, and bet heavily on her today."[46]

The last race of her career was a second in a one-mile race for horses of all ages at Sheepshead Bay. Finishing first by two lengths was the brilliant sprinter Hamburg Belle, the 6-5 favorite.

Molly Brant ended her career with nine wins, seven places and two shows from twenty-three starts. Her Saratoga record underlines her affinity for that track, with seventeen starts, seven wins, two places and no shows. Her only two wins outside Saratoga were her two-year-old handicap race at Gravesend and her 1903 Hunter Handicap at Brighton Beach. She defeated two future Hall of Fame inductees, Broomstick and Beldame, as well as such standouts as Africander, Reliable, Irish Lad and Major Daingerfield.

Molly Brant's career as a broodmare was short and unsuccessful. Her first foal, Chief Bartlett by Rockton, was born in 1907 and raced only three times in 1910, only beating one horse. Her other foal, Van Bu, by Chuctunuda, was born in 1908 and never raced.

Gritty Molly Brant, a favorite at Saratoga, died in 1908.

The Notorious Gottfried Walbaum

G ottfried Walbaum's impact on Saratoga cannot be overstated. While he was responsible for constructing what is the core of the distinctive grandstand that is America's oldest sports venue, he presided over the darkest period in the track's history. The quality of racing declined, he made some very unpopular changes and, after thirty-three uninterrupted seasons, the track was closed in 1896.

Walbaum was a gambler, promoter and entrepreneur who operated with at least one foot in the underworld. In his memoir, *Reminiscences of Gottfried Walbaum*, compiled in 1930–31 at the age of eighty-five, he said that he was born in Bremen, Germany, and immigrated to the United States to avoid serving in the military. However, America was moving toward the Civil War when he arrived in 1860, and he said he served in the U.S. Army and U.S. Navy during the conflict.

Following the war, Walbaum went to work in what he called a "sporting house" in New York City operated by Kit Burns, whose bar on Water Street in the Bowery featured the blood sports of dogfighting and rat-baiting. Patrons of Burns's club, the Band Box, bet on what animals and rodents would survive. Stories in the *New York Times* show that Burns also was involved in prizefighting.[47]

Walbaum said that he was in the business of selling fish before discovering gambling and providing protection to business owners. Although he said that he usually lost his money playing faro—one spectacular Saturday night, he dropped $24,000—he began acquiring gaming houses in the city and prospered. Faro was a very popular game in the nineteenth century in which people bet on cards being pulled from a standard deck of cards.

"Walking up the Bowery one night, there was a gambling house at the corner of Grand and Bowery," Walbaum noted in the memoirs compiled by Frank Tannehill. "I went up found they had a very small bankroll of about $500, and I bet them out of it and broke the gambling house. The man that owned it, his name was George McLeod, said to me, 'Well, want to buy it?' I asked him how much he wanted for it and he said, '$300.' So I said, 'I'll take it.' Now I had a gambling house at the corner of Grand Street and the Bowery and made plenty of money."[48]

In 1878, Walbaum moved into horse racing after a big win at Jerome Park in the Bronx; he cashed in on a $100 bet on a long shot facing the Hall of Fame horse Parole. "To make a long story short, General Phillips won and I got $2,100," he said in the memoirs. "So I said, 'By jinks, this is getting money easy. No use to work any more.' So from that, I was driven into the bookmaking business."[49]

Saratoga track president Gottfried Walbaum (third from left in second row) hosted New York governor Roswell P. Flower and the king of a region of India in 1893. *Courtesy of the Saratoga Springs History Museum.*

Walbaum moved into track management in 1887 as a partner in the Hudson County Racing Association, which ran the infamous Guttenberg track in northern New Jersey's Bergen County. The group expanded its new facility, a half-mile trotting track, into a one-mile track in 1889 with a glass-enclosed grandstand that could hold three thousand people and a big betting ring, the location where bookmakers conducted their business. Walbaum and his three partners were primarily interested in the gambling take and did not charge admission to the track. During that same period, Walbaum was a partner in a gambling house, the Arkansas Club, in the resort town of Hot Springs, Arkansas.

Guttenburg conducted racing in the winter when the tracks in New York were closed, giving it control of on-track and off-track betting. It quickly became notorious and was regularly criticized in the newspapers as the anti-gambling fervor grew in New Jersey. Not only did "The Gut" operate in the winter, which went against the grain in those years, but according to newspaper articles of the time, it also held races for two-year-olds very early in the year and was criticized for that practice. New Jersey banned winter racing in 1893.

At the end of 1891, the *New York Times* published a lengthy story titled "The Outlaws of the Turf," praising the work of the Racing Board of Control, precursor to The Jockey Club, for banning people who race at Guttenburg from the tracks it controls.[50] "Nothing has been done in the management of racing affairs in years has so much talk as the recent edict of the Racing Board of Control against the Guttenburg track. The consequences promise to be far-reaching and put the sport on a higher plane than any other action that could be taken. The board has done just the right thing, and there is no one that has the best interests of the sport at heart but acknowledge the fact."

However, by the time the Racing Board of Control came down on Guttenberg, Walbaum and his colleagues had acquired Saratoga Race Course, a far more prestigious track. A widely reported sale to a group of prominent businessmen and horse owners led by publisher W.J. Arkell fell through early in 1891, and Walbaum stepped into the picture that summer.

"Somebody informed me that Albert Spencer, who owned the Saratoga Track, wanted to sell it," Walbaum said in his memoirs. "I went and saw Spencer and he said he would sell out for $250,000. I had some friends there and asked them if they would like to go in with me—some of my old partners. But I had to take the biggest part of it. I owned 75 percent of the track stock, and 25 percent of it was taken by my friends."[51]

Walbaum's run in Saratoga debuted with the opening of the 1892 season and the new building complex of a grandstand, clubhouse and betting ring designed by the respected Boston architect Herbert Langford Warren. While Walbaum and his associates were in charge when the new facility opened several months later, authors Paul Roberts and Isabelle Taylor speculated in their 2011 book *The Spa: Saratoga's Legendary Race Course* that the plans for the new structure might have been put in place a year before the Guttenburg group arrived. The Arkell syndicate, which included August Belmont Sr. and Senator George Hearst, had made it clear that it intended major changes, but that sales agreement with Spencer did not last after Belmont died in November, Hearst died in February and Arkell retired from racing.[52]

By all accounts, Walbaum was a rough character who was full of himself. "He was given to loud boastings, and old-timers rate him second only to a celebrated bookie named Virginia Carroll as a user of profanity," Hugh Bradley wrote in *Such Was Saratoga*. However, Bradley added that the great trainer Sam Hildreth always defended Walbaum. "In truth, Walbaum seems to have been a crude, stubborn, vain and naive man who, according to his lights and within his limitations did the best he could."[53]

Walbaum didn't do Saratoga any favors, though. He changed the character of the competition at the track, and some of the older, more distinguished stables stayed away as sport gave way to what was considered corrupt racing and a focus on wagering. The hoodlums and gamblers who frequented Guttenberg were said to have followed him to Saratoga. They may have been coming before he arrived. Saratoga was, after all, a wide-open town, where just about anything was tolerated. During the Walbaum era, when an anti-gambling movement was trying to clean up America's most famous resort, they stood out.

John Cavanaugh, the longtime head of the bookmakers' organization that worked the New York tracks, recalled Walbaum during a 1936 interview in the New *York Evening Post*:

> *Walbaum was one of the oddest characters we ever had around the racetrack. He was a very stubborn fellow, always arguing with his men. They never did anything right.*
>
> *One of his men once held [sold] a tremendous amount on a favorite and the horse won [necessitating paying a lot of winning bettors]. Walbaum asked him the reason why and the layer said the horse was packing 124 pounds and he thought that was too much. Walbaum, on fire, shouted, "How do you know dot hawse carried 124*

Saratoga Springs, N.Y., Saratoga Race Track "The Start."

Flags and pennants fly from the top of the clubhouse and grandstand at historic Saratoga Race Course. *Courtesy of Victoria Garlanda.*

They're off at Saratoga in the days before the portable starting gate was introduced in 1940. *Courtesy of Victoria Garlanda.*

Two canoes were needed in 2012 when Alpha and Golden Ticket finished in a dead heat to win the Travers. *Photo by Mike Kane.*

Willy Beamin on the outside prevailed in the 2012 King's Bishop. *Photo by Mike Kane.*

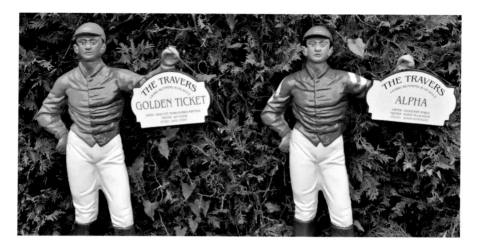

The morning after the 2012 Travers dead heat, two lawn jockeys were in position in the paddock. *Photo by Mike Kane.*

Godolphin's Questing was an impressive winner of the historic Alabama in 2012. *Photo by Mike Kane.*

Above: A sign over an entrance to the Jim Dandy bar provides a history lesson. *Photo by Mike Kane.*

Left: A blanket of pink carnations decorated the Sea Hero statue on Fabulous Fillies Day in 2012. *Photo by Mike Kane.*

Above: Red and white canopies and signs identify Saratoga Race Course. *Photo by Mike Kane.*

Right: Todd Pletcher has won a record-tying nine training titles at Saratoga. *Photo by Mike Kane.*

Flowers and jockey statues surround the fountain at the clubhouse entrance. *Photo by Mike Kane.*

An aerial image, probably from the 1930s, shows Saratoga Race Course and the Oklahoma training track in the background. *Courtesy of the Saratoga Springs Public Library/ Ed Hotaling Collection.*

A group of jockeys turns the rail into seating during a steeplechase race. *Courtesy of the Saratoga Springs Public Library/Ed Hotaling Collection.*

This view from the far turn near Union Avenue shows the betting ring and the grandstand. *Courtesy of Harry D. Snyder Esq.*

Steeplechase racing made its debut at Saratoga in 1864. *Courtesy of Victoria Garlanda.*

Hats for ladies and gents were in vogue in the Saratoga clubhouse. *Courtesy of Victoria Garlanda.*

Opposite, top: An admissions badge from the 1938 season. *Courtesy of Victoria Garlanda.*

Opposite, bottom: Saratoga's clubhouse and grandstand, with the distinctive roofline, opened in 1892. *Courtesy of Victoria Garlanda.*

An early twentieth-century postcard showing the judges' stand at the finish line. *Courtesy of Victoria Garlanda.*

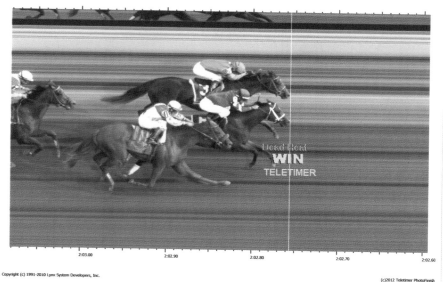

The photo-finish camera image shows that two noses were on the finish line of the 2012 Travers. *Courtesy NYRA/Don Morehouse.*

Clouds and sun create a distinctive late-afternoon sky. *Photo by Mike Kane.*

Rachel Alexandra and jockey Calvin Borel cast a big shadow during the post parade for the 2009 Woodward. *Photo by Mike Kane.*

The start of the 2009 Woodward, won by the filly Rachel Alexandra from post three. *Photo by Mike Kane.*

A wide-angle view of the clubhouse from the inside rail at the finish line. *Photo by Mike Kane.*

Next page, top: Four fillies were spread across the track in the stretch run of the 2012 Lake Placid. *Photo by Mike Kane.*

Next page, middle: To Honour and Serve and John Velazquez, inside, hold off Mucho Macho Man in the 2012 Woodward. *Photo by Mike Kane.*

Next page, bottom: America's oldest sports venue from the clubhouse turn. *Photo by Mike Kane.*

pounds?" Another day one of the layers held another favorite that won and Walbaum wanted to know the reason why. The layer said he had a report that the horse was coughing.

"Coughing!" Walbaum was about to wring his neck. "Dot hawse was laughing at you!"[54]

During his time at Saratoga, Walbaum cut purses, did not run established stakes like the Alabama and the Travers, allowed women and children to bet and moved the starting time of the races from 11:30 a.m. to 2:30 p.m., which infuriated the hotelkeepers. He ended the 1895 season early and, after a quarrel with The Jockey Club over dates, cancelled the 1896 season. Walbaum reopened Saratoga in 1897 and operated for four more seasons before selling to a group headed by William C. Whitney in 1900.

"Finally, the trouble I was having at Saratoga began to get on my nerves, and I did not sleep well nights, and my wife said to me, 'Fred, if I was you, I would sell out that track. You don't sleep sound and you wake up a dozen times a night.' I said, 'Mamma, all right, I'll sell it. I am going to sell it to Bill Wilden, the ex-Sheriff of Saratoga.'"[55]

Walbaum described how he went for a ride in Wilden's wagon and talked about getting rid of the track. "He asked, 'What do you want for it?'…I said, 'Well, I paid about a quarter million dollars for it. I built the grandstand, the Club House, and the other alterations cost about $125,000. At that rate, it makes about $375,000 invested.'"[56]

According to Walbaum in his memoirs, Wilden arranged the deal with Whitney and his partners. The transaction took place on Wall Street in New York.

Walbaum was fifty-five when he sold Saratoga Race Course. He continued in the gambling business in Manhattan. His most famous facility was at 31 West Thirty-third Street, a lavish layout designed by the famed architect Stanford White. One of the features was a seven-inch-thick bronze door built in the fifteenth century in Italy. Walbaum was reported to have paid $28,000 for the door and $25,000 for a hand-carved walnut staircase. By 1909, the casino had been closed by the authorities and was being turned into a restaurant.

In 1918, the contents of Walbaum's safe, containing many items and jewels that had been collateral for bettors, was auctioned in New York.[57] Two years after completing his rambling memoirs with Tannehill, Walbaum died on December 24, 1933.

East versus West in the 1879 Travers

Although largely forgotten today, the 1879 Travers was a race that *Daily Racing Form* said forty years later "fairly convulsed the racing world."[58] The outcome confirmed a new star.

The showdown at Saratoga featured two outstanding horses from different sections of the country: James R. Keene's Spendthrift, the best three-year-old colt of the East, against J.W. Hunt Reynolds's homebred Falsetto, the top three-year-old of the South and West, which in those days meant Kentucky and Illinois. While sectional rivalries have been abundant in American horse racing—Zenyatta and Rachel Alexandra are twenty-first-century examples—the 1879 Travers was particularly intense.

Spendthrift, a son of Australian by the Lexington mare Aerolite, was bred by Dan Swigert, who also owned him when he compiled a perfect five-for-five record as a two-year-old in 1878. Included in those wins were the Sandford at Churchill Downs and the Young American, as well as a sweepstakes for two-year-olds at Nashville. Finishing second in those last two races was Lord Murphy, who would be a prominent figure in the career of Falsetto.

The Thoroughbred Heritage named Spendthrift the co-champion two-year-old male of 1878 with George Lorillard's Harold, a son of Leamington. Harold's four-for-seven record included wins in the July Stakes at Monmouth, beating future handicap star Monitor; Saratoga's Flash, with Lord Murphy finishing eleventh; and the Saratoga Stakes.

After the 1878 season, Swigert sold Spendthrift to James Keene, the first of many champion horses that Keene would eventually own. Spendthrift

Spendthrift was the beaten favorite in the 1879 Travers. *Courtesy of the National Museum of Racing.*

started his 1879 season with a controversial second to his stablemate Dan Sparling in the Withers. Since entries had not yet been introduced into American racing, the custom at the time was for the owner to declare beforehand which horse he expected to win. Keene had declared Dan Sparling, so Spendthrift was held back, permitting the underdog stablemate to win the race, much to the consternation of the betting public. After the Withers, Spendthrift won the Belmont, the Lorillard and the Jersey Derby, giving him eight victories in nine career starts and making him the overwhelming favorite going into the Travers.

Harold opened his 1879 season with a win in the Preakness, then spent his next two races leading up to the Travers observing Spendthrift's posterior, finishing fourth to Spendthrift's controversial second in the Withers and a second to Spendthrift in the Lorillard. A surprising 2-5 favorite in the Withers, Harold lost all chance when he was left at the wire at the start.

The hero of the West, Falsetto, was by Enquirer out of Farfaletta by Australian. He did not race until his three-year-old season and began his career with a win in the Phoenix Hotel, followed by a second to Lord Murphy in the Kentucky Derby. That Derby loss would be the only blemish in Falsetto's brief racing career. Although one is tempted to ascribe his loss

Western invader Falsetto was the surprise winner of the 1879 Travers over Spendthrift. *Courtesy of the National Museum of Racing.*

at Churchill Downs to bad racing luck, in truth, the eventual winner had the most troubled trip when he almost went down after a collision with Ada Glenn. He was able to recover, beating Falsetto by a length. Falsetto probably was a better horse than Lord Murphy, but he was not the best on the day of the Kentucky Derby. Following his loss in the fifth running of the Derby, Falsetto rebounded one week later to win the Clark at Churchill Downs, his last race before his meeting with Spendthrift in the Travers.

On the day of the Travers, the stands were packed with spectators eager to see the coronation of Spendthrift as the best three-year-old in the country. According to the *New York Times*, "The sporting men were so confident that Spendthrift would win that it was difficult to secure any decent odds against him."[59] Even Falsetto's supporters were impressed with Spendthrift: "So great was the admiration expressed for [Spendthrift] that not a few Western enthusiasts declared that he was the greatest racer the country had ever produced."[60]

Falsetto, with Isaac Murphy aboard, took the early lead in the Travers, an advantage he did not relinquish, stunning the partisan crowd when he hit the wire two lengths ahead of Spendthrift. Finishing behind Spendthrift were Harold, Jericho and Dan Sparling.

"The blow was undoubtedly a hard one to Mr. Keene, who laid great hopes on securing the [Travers] trophy," the *Times* wrote.[61] The correspondent for the *Daily Tribune* was not ready to concede Falsetto's superiority: "One swallow does not make a Summer, however, nor does one race settle the question of superiority. Spendthrift's star has not set, though it is eclipsed for a time."[62]

If there was any doubt as to which was the better horse, Saratoga's Kenner Stakes on August 12 affirmed the superiority of Falsetto, who once again defeated Spendthrift by two lengths. This time, the eastern bettors made Falsetto the overwhelming favorite, aided by the rumors, apparently true, that the underdog had sore feet.

The Kenner was to be Falsetto's last race. After the Kenner, he was sold to Pierre Lorillard for $18,000 and sent to England to prepare for the 1880 season. Unfortunately, he broke down before his first race, in which he was to carry top weight of 129 pounds, and was retired. "It is related that his trials in England amazed the trainers of that country and to this day it is a question if a better American-bred horse ever cantered over New Market heath," the *Form* wrote.[63]

His name notwithstanding, Falsetto proved to be an excellent sire. Prominent among his get were Dew Drop and The Picket. Although some have noted that he sired three Kentucky Derby winners—Chant (1894), His Eminence (1901) and Sir Huon (1906)—all three won the Derby when it was in its thirty-year malaise.

Spendthrift's post-Saratoga season continued with a win in the Champion over Bramble and a second to Monitor in the Jerome. In 1880, Spendthrift followed Falsetto to England, but an illness delayed his debut until the fall, and after he finished fifth in the Cambridgeshire Handicap, he returned to the United States. He lost two purse events in 1881 and was retired to the breeding shed.

As good a sire as Falsetto was, he proved to be no match for Spendthrift, who became one of the top stallions of his generation. Among his best foals were future Hall of Fame inductee Kingston, Bankrupt, Lamplighter and Hastings, the latter of whom sired Fair Play, who in turn sired the great Man o' War.

Although Spendthrift's feats as a racehorse are remembered today by a relative handful of turf historians and fans, his name lives on with the iconic Spendthrift Farm in Lexington. It was originally established in 1937 by Dan Swigert's great-grandson, Leslie Combs II, who named it after Swigert's favorite horse. After a period of decline in the 1980s, it has been reinstated to its status as one of Kentucky's top stud farms and tourist attractions by its present owner, B. Wayne Hughes.

Things to Know About Saratoga

1. Histories of Saratoga racing correctly note that the three-year-old filly Lizzie W. was the winner of the first race held at opening Saratoga meeting in 1863. The second race of the day was won by Sympathy, the four-year-full sister of Lizzie W. They are by Scythian out of the Glencoe mare Prunella and were owned by Dr. J.W. Weldon.

   The sisters came back to win the two races on the fourth and final day of that first season. Sympathy took the first race on August 8 by sweeping a pair of one-mile heats from the five-year-old male John Morgan. Lizzie W. took the second race, 1¼-mile contest over two other fillies, the four-year-old Echo and the three-year-old Annie.

2. The Saratoga Special was a winner-take-all race from its inception in 1901 until 1959, when the conditions were changed to make it a standard stakes race. Twelve prominent horsemen agreed to underwrite the first running so it would have a minimum guaranteed value of $6,000. Others could nominate as many as three horses, but only one could start. The racing association did not put up money for the purse but agreed to pay $500 for a trophy. William C. Whitney's Goldsmith won the first running earning the purse of $15,500.

3. In addition to six seasons when the track was dark, racing has been cancelled a total of twenty-two days—twenty due to bad weather and twice as the result of the deaths of U.S. presidents.

The first time a full program was cancelled was August 21, 1871. Seventeen more days were cancelled through July 26, 1893. The next cancellation was more than one hundred years later, on August 2, 2006, due to intense heat that made it dangerous to race horses. The most recent cancellation was on Sunday, August 28, 2011, when what was left of Hurricane Irene swept through the Northeast.

On August 4, 1885, racing was cancelled because ex-president Ulysses S. Grant's body was transported through Saratoga on its way to Albany, where it was carried by train to New York City. Grant had died in nearby Wilton after completing his memoirs.

All sporting events in the country were cancelled on August 10, 1923, in honor of the recently deceased president Warren Harding, who was buried that day.

4. Now a Grade 1 sprint race, the Test was first run in 1922 as something of a do-over for the Alabama—hence the name. The race was staged as the result of Nedna's surprise Alabama victory on Thursday, August 10. Nedna prevailed in the stretch when the even-money favorite Emotion tired to capture the 1¼-mile race by one and a half lengths. Harry Payne Whitney's Pruddish, coupled in the wagering with Nedna, was another one and a half lengths back in third in the five-horse race.

Four days later, the *New York Times* reported that a rematch had been scheduled. "Since the running of the Alabama Stakes, the classic of the meeting for three-year-old fillies, there has been considerable discussion as to whether Nedna, the winner, was the best horse in the race."[64]

The *Times* story noted that the Saratoga Association wanted to bring the Alabama field back together and would offer a purse of $1,500 for a race for fillies at 1¼ miles on Wednesday, August 30.

Nedna, Emotion and Pruddish were entered in the Test, but Pruddish scratched, producing a match race. Nedna opened a two-length lead on the backstretch, but Emotion pulled even on the far turn. When jockey Linus "Pony" McAtee asked for more from Emotion in the stretch, she pulled away to a one-and-a-half-length victory.

In 1926, the Test was brought back at its current seven-furlong distance. Jockey Earl Sande guided J.E. Widener's Ruthenia to a victory by a head over the odds-on favorite, Corvette.

5. Hall of Fame trainer Jonathan Sheppard extended his personal winning streak at Saratoga to forty-four years in 2012. Sheppard had one win in 1967

but was blanked in 1968. He won twice in 1969 and picked up at least one win through the next four-plus decades. He led the trainers' standings in 1984 and 1985. Sheppard, the leading steeplechase trainer in American history, has won many flat races during his career.

Fellow Hall of Famers, A.J. Joyner, Sunny Jim Fitzsimmons and Phil Johnson are among the trainers who had extremely long and successful careers at Saratoga Race Course. H. Allen Jerkens has been winning races at Saratoga in his name since 1951.

6. Kelso won the Whitney three times, but the first victory, in 1961, came at Belmont Park. His 1963 and 1965 Whitneys came at Saratoga. The New York Racing Association moved the Whitney to Belmont, association chairman John W. Hanes said, because there were too many distance races at Saratoga. Hanes said it was a decision made by racing secretary Jimmy Kilroe.

Top: Hall of Fame trainer Jonathan Sheppard extended his Saratoga winning streak to forty-four years in 2012. *Photo by Mike Kane.*

Right: H. Allen Jerkens saddled his first Saratoga winner in 1951 and has competed at the track in seven decades. *Courtesy of the Maryland Jockey Club.*

"He said that it was done as a means of balancing up the NYRA program, insofar as distances are concerned," Hanes said in an interview with Landon Manning.[65]

Kelso finished second but was declared the winner when Our Hope was disqualified by the stewards. Kelso was carrying 130 pounds, 19 more than Our Hope, who set a stakes record of 1:48.

7. John Campo turned a racing oddity when the veteran trainer swept the top three spots in the 1976 Adirondack Stakes with Harvest Girl, Bonnie Empress and Drama Critic.

8. Trainer Linda Rice took it a step further on August 18, 2008, when she saddled the top four finishers in the $83,250 Mechanicville Stakes, a turf sprint. Rice won the race with Ahvee's Destiny, who finished a head in front of Canadian Ballet. Silver Timber was half a length farther back in third and Karakorum Elektra another three-quarters of a length behind in fourth.

9. Hundreds of young horses headed to greatness have stepped out onto the big stage at Saratoga Race Course. Yet, on August 13, 1968, a rarity occurred: two future Hall of Famers raced in the same race as maidens, with Ta Wee winning and Shuvee finishing fifth.

Only two other times in American Thoroughbred history have two future Hall of Fame inductees run in the same race as maidens. On September 6, 1925, at Belmont Park, Jolly Roger finished first and Fairmount second in a three-years-and-up maiden steeplechase event. Almost eight years later, on June 28, 1933, at Arlington Park, Cavalcade finished third and Discovery fifth in a maiden special weight race won by Singing Wood.

10. One of Saratoga's oldest and most prestigious races, the Grade 1 Spinaway, was named for George Lorillard's brilliant two-year-old filly, who never raced at Saratoga. Spinaway won seven of nine starts in 1880, all of them in stakes at Jerome Park, Monmouth Park and Gravesend. Spinaway was retired in 1881 due to an injury, and a race was run in her honor that year.

11. Lots of people refer to the Travers as the Mid-Summer Derby, but they may not know why. For three years, 1927–29, the official name of the Travers was changed to the Travers Mid-Summer Derby. The original name was restored before the Jim Dandy shocker of 1930.

12. Irish Linnet earned a place in Saratoga history when she won the Yaddo for New York breds for five consecutive years, 1991–95. She was trained by Leo O'Brien for Austin Delaney.

13. William Bird trained the winners of seven of the eight races held during the inaugural 1863 meeting. The African American horseman won the Kentucky Derby and Clark Handicap in 1884, the year he died. Among his many other accomplishments was an upset victory over Hindoo with Crickmore.

Three Equine Meteors

A lthough there have been several horses that have won four stakes in a season at Saratoga, there were three two-year-olds that equaled or bettered this feat but were rarely heard from again. Their brilliance was brief.

Novelty, a 1908 foal by Hall of Fame inductee Kingston out of Curiosity by the British import Voter, was the most accomplished horse of the trio. He was originally owned by future Hall of Fame inductee John Madden, trained by S. Walker and bred by James Keene. After he broke his maiden at Belmont in his first career start, he was sold to another future Hall of Famer, Sam Hildreth, who was to be his owner and trainer for the rest of his career in the United States.

Before heading to Saratoga for the 1910 season, Novelty went to the post nine times, winning five races and placing in two others, none of them stakes. On August 2, he won an allowance race at Saratoga, with the bettors making him the 3-5 favorite. He was entered in his first stakes race on August 10 in the United States Hotel, finishing third as the 8-5 favorite to 4-1 Naushon, with Iron Mask finishing second. This would be the last time in his career that Novelty finished behind those two rivals.

On August 13, Novelty won the Saratoga Special at 10-1, with Iron Mask again finishing second at odds of 5-2 and Naushon third as the 4-5 favorite. Four days later, he beat Textile easily in a special race that turned out to be a match race (Horizon was also entered but was scratched). Textile had previously won the overnight Hurricana Stakes and the Albany Handicap at Saratoga. Novelty continued his winning ways on August 20 when he took

Samuel Hildreth (*right*), with August Belmont, owned and trained Novelty. *Courtesy of the National Museum of Racing.*

the Hopeful, with Iron Mask second and Naushon third. This was followed on August 27 by a win in the Rensselaer Handicap, with Naushon second and Textile third.

The last day of the Saratoga meeting, on August 31, 1910, produced a historical oddity. The state legislature had recently passed the Executive Liability Act, which made track executives liable for illegal bets accepted at their tracks, which effectively ended betting on horse races in New York State. Since the law was to go into effect on September 1, when the rich Futurity was scheduled to be run at Sheepshead Bay, the race was moved to Saratoga, the only time that race was held at the Spa.

The Futurity had a field of twelve, including the usual suspects Novelty, Textile, Naushon and Iron Mask. Entered with Novelty was Zeus, who prior to the Futurity had won Saratoga's Adirondack Handicap. Facing Novelty for the first time was Bashti, a filly who, after losing the first race of her career, had won five races in a row, including the Criterion, Astoria, Vernal and Spinaway Stakes. Following the Spinaway, Bashti's owner, Newcastle Farms, sold her to Harry Payne Whitney for $30,000. The entry of Novelty and Zeus went off as the slight favorite at 9-5, with Bashti the second choice at 5-2. The filly Love-Not, a 20-1 shot owned by E.R. Bradley, was the pacesetter through most of the race before she was collared by Novelty in the stretch, the latter winning handily. Finishing second was a game Bashti, who recovered from a bad start. Love-Not held on for third.

Novelty, with Carroll Schilling aboard, completed a brilliant 1910 season with a win in the Futurity. *Courtesy of the Keeneland Library.*

As a further indication of Novelty's ability, Iron Mask, whom Novelty beat in three of their four encounters, would return from England in 1913 and become one of the country's leading sprinters. Iron Mask won four of six races in 1913, but the highlight of his career came in Juarez, Mexico, on January 4, 1914, when he beat future Hall of Famer Pan Zareta. In that two-horse, six-furlong race, Iron Mask set a new record for the distance.

By winning the Futurity, "Novelty stamped himself as the best two-year-old of 1910," proclaimed *Daily Racing Form*, adding that "it was won by a colt that by his previous deeds had made himself the most popular horse that raced during the long Saratoga meeting."[66] In the same story, *Daily Racing Form* anointed Bashti as the best two-year-old filly in the country, an honor that was affirmed when she concluded her season with a win in Pimlico's Matron Stakes.

Novelty had by far the most earnings of any two-year-old in the country in 1910, winning a total of $72,630, with Bashti finishing a distant second with $27,235. Perhaps Novelty's highest accolade came from his breeder, the legendary Keene, who was quoted in *Daily Racing Form* as having told Hildreth, "I believe you have the greatest horse in the world....He can go fast and far, and he handles weight as easily as a horse twice his size might. I am sorry I did not keep him, but since it was not my fortune to have him win for me, I do not know of anyone I'd rather he had won for than you."

The story continues by quoting Hildreth as saying, "He is certainly the greatest horse I ever owned or handled."[67] This praise came from a man who had already trained champions Spendthrift, Jean Bereaud, Fitz Herbert and Admiration. For the record, in 1910 Novelty had eleven wins, two seconds and two thirds in sixteen starts. His record at Saratoga was six wins and one third from seven starts, four of those wins coming in stakes.

One can only speculate what Novelty might have accomplished if New York hadn't shut down horse racing in the state. He had an abbreviated season in 1911, winning three of four purse races in Canada and one purse race at Pimlico. His old foe Naushon finished third to his second in his only loss in Canada and third in Novelty's win at Pimlico.

After his 1911 season, Novelty and all of Hildreth's other horses were sold to Charles Kohler, who retained Hildreth as his trainer and shipped both to England and, eventually, to France for the 1912 season. Considering that he had to adapt to a new environment and surface, Novelty did not disgrace himself in France. After finishing eleventh in the F100,000 Grand Prix de Deauville on August 18, he won two lesser events, the F25,000 Handicap de la Tamise at Maisons-Laffitte and the F15,000 Prix de l'Escault at the same track.

Acting on orders from Kohler, Hildreth trained Novelty to be a steeplechaser. From November 19 through December 12, 1912, he won two of six jumping events. He continued to run in steeplechases in 1915, compiling a record of one win, one second and two thirds in four starts. The most impressive result was a second in the rich F50,000 Prix de Monte Carlo on January 5 at Nice.

Apparently, the jumping experiment was deemed a failure, and on September 24, 1913, Novelty returned to the flat track to finish in a dead heat for first with Chut in the F6,000 Prix de Danube at Maisons-Laffitte. In his career finale, he was fifth in the F100,000 Prix du Conseil Municipal in Paris on October 5, 1913. In 1914, he began what appears to have been a successful stud career in Brazil.[68]

Although Novelty disappeared from the limelight after his successful 1910 season, he may possibly be the only American-bred horse that won races in three different counties and on dirt, turf and over hurdles.

In 1936, an unheralded two-year-old colt named Maedic burst onto the scene at Saratoga. Out of the Campfire mare Little Fire by Bostonian, he was owned by DeWitt Page's Maemere Farm, trained by George E. Phillips and bred by A.B. Gordon. Before coming to Saratoga, he had raced a demanding sixteen times at Hialeah, Tropical Park, Belmont, Aqueduct and Empire City, winning three races, none of them stakes. His ability to handle the rigorous schedule was a reflection of his Bonnie Scotland-Bramble-Ben Brush male line.[69] On July 1, as a hint of things to come, he finished third in Aqueduct's Great American Stakes to the favorite, Fairy Hill, and two lengths behind the second-place finisher, a horse named War Admiral.

Maedic began his remarkable season at Saratoga on July 29 by winning the Flash as the 5-2 favorite. He followed that with wins in the Saratoga Sales Stakes on August 4, the Sanford on August 13, the Grand Union Hotel on August 22 and the Hopeful on August 29. Although the competition in his earlier efforts was hardly imposing, in the Hopeful he faced E.R. Bradley's Billionaire, who had beaten Maedic earlier in the Wakefield Handicap at Empire City and had tuned up for the Hopeful on August 19 with a five-length allowance win at Saratoga.

Billionaire might have been the favorite on a dry track, but a heavy rain the day of the Hopeful made the track sloppy, favoring Maedic based on his win in the Grand Union on a muddy track. The bettors made Maedic the slight favorite at 9-5, with Billionaire the second favorite at 5-2. Maedic showed the wisdom of the crowd by catching the front-running Billionaire at the three-sixteenths pole, winning the Hopeful by an emphatic five lengths and putting the cap on a perfect five-for-five season at Saratoga.

John Hervey wrote, "It may be said that in every one of these races [at Saratoga] Maedic outclassed his field completely...Taken as a whole, the five acts in the drama were played with a style and power that left the star actor, as he bowed in the spotlight, the whole show."[70]

Despite Maedic's successful season at Saratoga, two-year-old male horse honors for 1936 went to Pompoon, winner of the National Stallion and Futurity Stakes and leading money winner in his division. Maedic's cause was not aided when his post-Saratoga races resulted in a fifth to War Admiral in the Eastern Shore and a fourth in the Remsen.

Maedic's skein at Saratoga was tainted, probably unfairly, when trainer George E. Phillips was indefinitely suspended two days after the Grand Union Hotel because an illegal substance was found in one of his other horses. Maedic was put under the care of another trainer, Jack Whyte, who was the trainer of record when Maedic won the Hopeful. Although Phillips was reinstated six weeks later, the taint probably lingered.

The rest of Maedic's career was lackluster at best, winning one of four races in 1937 and two of eight in 1938. None of his wins was in stakes events.

The last member of the shining juvenile trio is Devil's Thumb, a 1940 foal by Grand Slam out of the Blue Larkspur mare Daintiness. He was owned by airplane manufacturer W.E. Boeing, trained by C.W. Wilhelm and bred by Lucas Combs.

Devil's Thumb began his career in less-than-spectacular fashion, losing his first nine races before breaking his maiden on July 17 at Arlington Park. Ten days later, he made his debut in Saratoga in the Flash, finishing second to Breezing Home at odds of 6.15-1 on a sloppy track. The Flash was the last time he would lose at Saratoga, as he won the United States Hotel, Saratoga Sales, Sanford, Grand Union Hotel and Hopeful. After being made the second choice in the Grand Union Hotel with his stablemate, Corona, he was the favorite in his last four races, including the prestigious Hopeful at 1-2.

A weak ankle kept him on the sidelines for the rest of the season, preventing him from proving his mettle against the two top colts of his division, future Triple Crown winner Count Fleet and Occupation. Injuries also sidelined him in 1943 and 1944, and he ended his career ignominiously when he was eased shortly after the start in the 1945 Roseben.

Like Maedic, Devil's Thumb never met the best of his division, making it difficult to assess his ability. What will remain, however, is his magical four weeks in which he won five of six stakes at Saratoga.

A History of the Saratoga Cup

In 1865, one year after the Saratoga Race Course opened and the first Travers was run, the Saratoga Association inaugurated the Saratoga Cup for horses of all ages at a distance of 2¼ miles. The length of the race seems extraordinarily long today but was normal in the nineteenth century. For many years, the Saratoga Cup was one of the most prestigious races of the annual summer meeting.

A measure of a race's reputation is the quality of horses that have competed in it, and by that standard, the Saratoga Cup has to be considered one of the most prominent stakes races for older horses in the country. In its seventy-five-year history, the Saratoga Cup was won twenty times by horses that have been inducted into the Hall of Fame: Kentucky (winner of the first two Saratoga Cups in 1865 and 1866), Longfellow (1871), Harry Bassett (1872), Parole (1877, 1878), Beldame (1904), Roamer (1915), Exterminator (1919–22), Reigh Count (1928), Gallant Fox (1930), Twenty Grand (1931), Equipoise (1933), Granville (1936), War Admiral (1938) and Stymie (1945, 1946). Nine other Hall of Fame inductees failed in the Cup.

Other outstanding horses who have won the Cup include Muggins (1867), a long-forgotten campaigner who compiled a twelve-race winning streak, mainly in the South; Helmbold (1870); Joe Daniels (1873); Springbok (1874 and 1875, the latter a dead heat with Preakness); Tom Ochiltree (1876); Thora (1882); Volante (1886); Los Angeles (1891); Africander (1903); Friar Rock (1916); Omar Khayyam (1917); Johren (1918); and Diavolo (1929).

The Saratoga Cup was held without interruption from its original running in 1865 through 1886. Then, with the exception of 1891, it lay dormant from 1887 until 1901, when the track was purchased from the notorious Gottfried Walbaum by a syndicate headed by William C. Whitney.

With Whitney's group in control, the race was restored. With the exception of 1908, when half the track's schedule was lost to the newly established Empire City Race Track in Yonkers, and 1911 and 1912, when the track was closed, it was held every year until its demise after the 1955 season.

It was held at Belmont Park from 1943 through 1945, when Saratoga was closed due to World War II travel restrictions. The original $2\frac{1}{4}$-mile distance was shortened to 2 miles in 1891 and was further shortened to $1\frac{5}{8}$ miles when the race was restored in 1901. In 1902, a furlong was added, and the $1\frac{3}{4}$-mile distance remained until the race was abandoned, at least on the dirt. A variation was resurrected briefly in later years.

The Cup was designated a weight-for-age race in 1901 and retained that qualification for the remainder of its existence. For the years 1927, 1928, 1931, 1932 and 1946 through 1955, geldings were not eligible.

One of the most celebrated races in the history of the Saratoga Cup was the 1872 edition, which featured two future Hall of Fame inductees: Longfellow, the first popular racehorse of the post–Civil War era and the winner of the previous year's Saratoga Cup, and Harry Bassett. A third horse, Defender, was also entered, but he was given no chance by the spectators, and he ran to that billing. In 1871, Harry Bassett was a sensation as a three-year-old when he won all nine of his races, including the Belmont, Travers and Kenner. He continued his winning ways in 1872 until he ran into the five-year-old Longfellow in the much-anticipated $2\frac{1}{2}$-mile Monmouth Cup in New Jersey. That race became anticlimactic when Longfellow was so far ahead after $1\frac{1}{4}$ miles that Harry Bassett sulked the rest of the way.

Two weeks later, the two met again in the Saratoga Cup, and this time Harry Bassett won, leading from start to finish despite a desperate effort by Longfellow to close the gap. Not only did Harry Bassett win by one length, but he also set a new world record for the distance. However, what made the race so remarkable was that at the beginning of the race, Longfellow flipped his shoe, mutilating his left heel. Despite racing $2\frac{1}{4}$ miles as a virtual cripple, he forced his younger opponent to extend himself to his fullest to win. It was Longfellow's last race, and it was his gallant losing effort that would make him a legend.

Other prominent editions of the Saratoga Cup include the dead heat between Springbok and Preakness in 1875; the 1903 victory of Africander by a nose over Heno, with the favorite, Waterboy, a distant third; the 1904

Longfellow, with owner John Harper, turned in a gallant effort in a loss in the 1872 Saratoga Cup. *Courtesy of the National Museum of Racing.*

running in which the three-year-old filly sensation and 1955 Hall of Fame inductee Beldame won by six lengths over such male stalwarts as Africander, The Picket and Caughnawaga; the 1916 win by that year's three-year-old male champion Friar Rock over handicap star and future Hall of Famer Roamer and the favorite in the race, The Finn; the emotional 1922 win by the popular gelding Exterminator, who won his fourth Saratoga Cup in a row by narrowly defeating two-time Metropolitan Handicap and Jockey Club Gold Cup winner Mad Hatter; and the 1936 renewal, which became a match race between two future Hall of Fame inductees, the five-year-old handicap star Discovery and the brilliant three-year-old Granville. Youth was served with Granville winning by a resounding eight lengths.

After Granville's victory, the race went into what was to be an irreversible decline, possibly because of its anachronistic distance, the weight-for-age condition, which caused owners of weaker horses from entering, or a surfeit of races for older horses. War Admiral (1938) and Stymie (1945 and 1946) were future Hall of Fame inductees who won the race after Granville, but their competition was mediocre at best and, in the case of Stymie's 1946 walkover win, none at all.

Exterminator dominated the Saratoga Cup with four consecutive victories from 1919 to 1922. *Courtesy of the National Museum of Racing.*

The winner of the 1951 and 1952 editions, the Phipps family's filly/ mare Busanda, was never close to being a champion, her claim to fame being the dam of the immortal Buckpasser. The last three winners of the Cup—Alerted (1953), Great Captain (1954) and Chevation (1955)—could probably not be identified by the most astute turf historians.

In 1963, the New York Racing Association held a one-time-only event called "The seventy-sixth running Saratoga Cup 'The Centennial Season Running.'" It was held on the turf course at a distance of 1⅝ miles. The winner was F.E. Dixon's Will I Rule, who earlier in the meet had won the Promise Hurdle Handicap at Saratoga.

In 1988, the New York Racing Association began what was called the Saratoga Breeders' Cup Handicap on the turf. It was dropped the next year and then resumed in 1993 and continued through 2004. Although some sources have called this race a continuation of the Saratoga Cup, in this case the cup in the title referred to the race's sponsor, the Breeders' Cup, and has no relation to its more illustrious predecessor.

Gates Closed on Union Avenue

In 2013, Saratoga Springs celebrates the 150th anniversary of the start of Thoroughbred racing in the city before, during and after what is its 145th season. For three different reasons, Saratoga Race Course was closed for a total of six summers, so the 150th season will take place in 2018.

The three breaks have a progression: the single season of 1896; two years, 1911–12; and finally, three seasons, 1943, 1944 and 1945. There was no connection to the closings other than the fear in Saratoga Springs that racing, which was so important to the economy and a part of a culture, would be gone forever.

In 1896, the controversial ownership group, which was under fire for the way it was running the track, decided not to accept the dates offered by The Jockey Club and did not open. The 1911–12 gap was the result of anti-gambling legislation enacted by New York State. Restrictions in travel during World War II kept the track shuttered, while the Saratoga Racing Association conducted its season at Belmont Park.

By the mid-1890s, anti-gambling forces were trying to clean up Saratoga Springs, which had developed a reputation as a wide-open town. The crusading journalist Nellie Bly blistered Saratoga in a lengthy article, "Our Wickedest Summer Resort," in the *New York World* on August 19, 1894.[71] The subheads, including "The Shameful Story of the Vice and Crime, Dissipation and Profligacy at This Once Most Respectable Watering-Place," set the tone for her exposé of Saratoga. Bly started swinging in the opening paragraphs:

Grass grew on the track during the three-year closing for World War II. *Courtesy of the Saratoga Room, Saratoga Public Library.*

> *Saratoga is the wickedest spot in the United States.*
>   *Crime is holding a convention there and vice is enjoying a festival such as it never dare approach before.*
>   *I was told so, I rather doubted it, and I went there to see.*

Bly described a visit to the racetrack, where there was a special room for women to wager, and she saw many children in the stands. She interviewed Caleb Mitchell, the president of the village, who operated a gambling house across Broadway from the United States Hotel. One of the subheads on the story referred to Gottfried Walbaum, the majority owner of Saratoga Race Course, as "Czar Walbaum."

The 1894 season was Walbaum's third in control of Saratoga racing. His approach, developed during the years running the infamous Guttenberg track in northern New Jersey, was criticized from the start. In its review of the 1892 season, the *New York Times* gave Walbaum's track a mixed grade: "The races have been considered fair this season. There have been some objectionable features to them, notably that of the betting room for women.

The spectacle of seventy-five women crowding into a small apartment to bet from 25 cents to $500 was not edifying, and has never in past seasons been deemed necessary."[72]

The article also noted that the Walbaum syndicate was attempting to purchase the Leach cottage on the corner of Union Avenue and Circular Street as a site for a casino to compete with the casino—the Club House, now known as the Canfield Casino—operated by Albert Spencer.

John Morrissey—the former boxer, gang leader, gambling hall owner and congressman credited with starting racing in Saratoga Springs in 1863—opened the Saratoga Club House in 1870. When Morrissey died at the age of forty-seven in May 1878, Spencer and Charles Reed, his partners in the 5 West Twenty-fourth Street gambling house in New York, took over the Saratoga properties.[73] Reed ran the track, and Spencer handled the gambling and the Club House. In 1887, Reed sold out to Spencer.[74] Author Ed Hotaling said that Reed got out because he was being snubbed by Saratoga society and was harassed by the crusaders.[75]

Saratoga Race Course was in operation at the conclusion of the Civil War, but several other tracks opened in New York City and New Jersey in the following years and were vying for horses and racing dates. Spencer Trask, the Wall Street financier, had purchased an estate in Saratoga Springs just to the east of the track and was determined to clean up Saratoga. He spent a lot of money putting pressure on the town and the gamblers.[76]

Spencer continued to run the track and the casino, but in August 1890, printed reports noted that he was planning to sell the track.[77] The names August Belmont and Pierre Lorillard were mentioned in the story as partners in a group headed by publisher W.J. Arkell.

"The sale of the race track, now an accepted and established fact, puts a new phase on the gambling question here," the *Times* story reported. "In this connection, Mr. W.J. Arkell, who represents the syndicate of purchasers, says: 'I do not wish to be quoted as attacking or reflecting on Mr. Spencer or his pursuits. It is none of my concern and I have no information as to his intentions. But the public may rest assured that the new Saratoga Jockey Club will have no connection with any gambling business.'"

Arkell went on to say that the separation of the racetrack from the Club House would cost Spencer public support. In fact, that is what happened. Without the clout of being able to threaten to close the track if the authorities closed the casino, Spencer became vulnerable. He had been arrested for operating a gambling house twice in 1889,[78] and he was arrested again in the following years as the anti-gambling efforts gained momentum.

The deal to sell the track to the Arkell group did not take place when two of the principals, Belmont and Senator George Hearst, died and Arkell retired from the sport. Spencer operated the track, but by the end of the 1891 season, the sale to Walbaum and his associates had been completed. Hearst's death changed the course of history at Saratoga. Instead of the association being taken over by wealthy sportsmen, it fell into the hands of a group that was more concerned with controlling and profiting from gambling.

Change was underway in Saratoga Springs. On May 20, 1893, the *Johnstown Daily Republican* reported that Spencer had sold 50 percent of the Club House to the noted gambling house owner Richard Canfield. By the next year, Canfield had complete control of the nation's most famous casino, and Spencer had moved to France.

The *New York Times* reported in the summer of 1892 that Walbaum had gained majority control by buying out one of his Guttenberg partners, Dennis McLaughlin, who was a political leader in Hudson County, New Jersey, and provided the protection from law enforcement.

Walbaum and associates took control of the track. In his memoirs, he noted that he paid $250,000 for the property, but there are published reports that it went for $375,000.[79] He made a series of changes, including opening a betting area for women and changing the staring time for the races from 11:30 a.m. to 2:30 p.m., which infuriated the local businessmen who had developed a schedule for visitors that included spending middays at the track and returning to the hotels for large meals. In addition, the Walbaum group dropped a number of historic stakes, like the Alabama and the Saratoga Cup, as it moved toward cheaper purses.

By January 1894, the newly formed Jockey Club and the horsemen in New York sought assurances from the Saratoga group that it would conduct honest racing and under the same terms in the city. Walbaum's representative agreed, and a thirty-day meet was held, running from July 23 through August 25.[80]

Racing continued to deteriorate in Saratoga, and by 1895, The Jockey Club was flexing its muscle by assigning dates to New York City tracks that conflicted with Saratoga. At the same time, reformers had gained strength, Bly's story had been published and laws had been passed that prohibited gambling in Saratoga Springs. Due to the legislation, Canfield and the other gambling operators closed in 1895. Gambling was affected at the track because the betting ring where the bookmakers did their business was closed, and bets had to be made on credit away from the grounds. Business was so bad at the track that the season was shortened from the scheduled forty days to twenty-eight. Some reports said that Walbaum wanted to close on August 7, but association president Edward Kearney would not allow that to happen, and the season ran through August 23.[81]

The August 11 edition of the *Times* noted that it was understood that racing would not be held the next year.[82]

The Jockey Club reserved dates from July 1 through August 15 for Saratoga, but the 1896 season was cancelled during a meeting of the Saratoga Association's Executive Committee on Saturday, January 25, as reported in the *Spirit of the Times* for February 1, 1896: "Resolved that there will be no racing in Saratoga in 1896, the reason being that the dates allotted by the Jockey Club were short of the just number due. Formerly, the month of August, up to and including the 24th was given to the association, but this year the Coney Island Jockey Club commences on the 15th. That being the case, the horses and jockeys will leave our track. The dates allotted give to us only 11 racing days in August without conflict. This leaves the association no other alternative other than to cancel the meeting or to sustain a heavy loss."

Two days before the season was cancelled, the association wrote to The Jockey Club, asking that the Coney Island opening be pushed back to at least August 21, which is still earlier than the opening for Sheepshead Bay on August 24 in 1895. After The Jockey Club responded, saying that it considered the request but that no change would be made, the *Spirit of the Times* commented: "The action of the Saratoga Association is to be regretted, as horses always improve during their stay at the Springs, and the summer colony takes a lively interest in the sport. Under the new conditions, it hardly seems probable that a meeting of lengthy duration could be made a financial success. Certainly the experience of the summer of 1895 would justify one of arriving at such a conclusion."

Racing returned on July 28, 1897, but there was some overlap with the New York City tracks, and the twenty-two-day meet closed on August 21. Walbaum continued to operate at Saratoga for three more seasons amid increasing criticism. By that point, the selling of entries and results to poolrooms that were illegal off-track betting sites in cities across the country through the telegraph was an important source of revenue.

In November 1900, the *New York Times* reported the sale of Saratoga Race Course to a group headed by William C. Whitney. The transaction completed what was the darkest era in the track's history.[83]

Whitney and his associates spent $1 million on their new racing property, and it was ready for the 1902 season. The changes included expanding the track to its current configuration of 1⅛ miles, adding the seven-furlong chute, a now-gone 1-mile chute, a grass course, shifting the direction of the building to avoid the afternoon sun shining in the faces of spectators and a new betting ring.

Nine years later, the track closed following the 1910 season, and it looked like racing might be doomed. Anti-gambling legislation pushed by Governor Charles Evans Hughes, a native of nearby Glens Falls, had been in place for a few years, but it didn't have the teeth to withstand challenges. In his speech to the legislature that year, the end of his second term as governor, Hughes insisted that the state Senate and Assembly make the changes necessary so that the racetrack regulations in the state's penal code would be in line with the state constitution's ban on professional gambling. Gambling was illegal at the time, of course, but it was not being enforced. Hughes was determined to make the changes that would stop gambling.

Hughes wasn't exactly popular with the citizenry of Saratoga Springs, with his anti-gambling campaign that became the Hart-Agnew Law, which was passed in special session of the legislature on June 11, 1908. The deciding vote for the Hart-Agnew bill was cast by Brooklyn senator Otto G. Foelker during an extraordinary session in Albany. The racing interests had thought that Foelker was on their side, but he voted for the bills, which ended up stalled by a deadlock—twenty-five votes even. When they were brought back and the extraordinary session called, Foelker was recovering from surgery. He made the trip back to Albany by train with his doctor and a nurse, was taken by ambulance to his residence and was given police protection. He arrived at the capitol the next day in time for the vote and was half carried to his seat.

The statute was challenged in court, and it was ruled that the legislation did not prevent oral betting, so racing continued. It came to a halt at the conclusion of the Saratoga meeting on August 31, 1910, because new legislation, prohibited all types of wagering, including oral bets. More important, another provision, the Executive Liability Act, made the directors of the track culpable if any illegal activity took place, even if they didn't know about it. Adding directors like August Belmont II to the equation led to the closing of the tracks.[84]

Saratoga lost its economic engine, and members of the Saratoga Association worked to change the legislation. Hope for a 1911 season lingered into the summer. In August, officials of the association opened the grounds to the public.

A decision on October 1912 by State Supreme Court justice Townsend Scudder of Nassau County, ruling that Paul Shane was not guilty of bookmaking at a United Hunts meeting at Belmont Park, enabled racing to return. It was a technicality more than anything, but Scudder said that the liability law could not be enforced.[85]

Racing resumed the following year, and Saratoga reopened on August 2, 1913. The response was enthusiastic. The *Saratogian* predicted a spirited return of the sport, but remarkably, it carried a sidebar story on an inside page noting that it was the forty-ninth anniversary of the start of racing in Saratoga Springs. The paper failed to include the inaugural 1863 season, so the rebirth of racing on Union Avenue actually was one day shy of the fiftieth anniversary. However, the subhead on the first page was correct in its prediction of a lively opener: "Historic Course Will Be Crowded When the Barrier Goes Up. Attractive Program Offered Enthusiasts for the First Day's Racing Here Since 1910."[86]

The report in the *New York Times* estimated that a crowd of seven thousand was at the old track. The Flash Stakes was won by Old Rosebud, who went on to win the 1914 Kentucky Derby in a Hall of Fame career.

"Racing returned to Saratoga Springs to-day," the *Times* wrote, "with much of the glory that made the village the Mecca for racing folk for almost half a century. For two years the association had been unable to open its gates by reason of the anti-betting laws, and the enthusiasm that prevailed with the return of the thoroughbreds spoke volumes for the popularity of the sport."[87]

Racing continued without interruption in Saratoga for thirty more years—many of them glorious seasons featuring racing's biggest stars—but was stopped for what turned out to be three years by World War II. America quickly responded to the Japanese attack on Pearl Harbor on December 7, 1941, and was also soon involved in Europe and North Africa. Despite fears that Saratoga might be closed, Saratoga Association president George Bull announced in May that the 1942 season would be held as scheduled. The thirty-day meeting closed on August 29 in front of crowd of 14,300.

It took several months before the government officially said that Saratoga would not be open in 1943. New York governor Thomas Dewey said on March 13 that he approved the report of his executive assistant, James C. Hagerty, that the Saratoga dates be run at New York metropolitan tracks. Hagerty was complying with a directive from federal rubber administrator William Jeffers urging the closing of tracks that could be reached only by automobile.

Saratogians, led by longtime mayor Addison Mallery, pushed back and made the argument that racing should continue. Mallery's group contended that Saratoga was a health resort and that people would walk to the track.

The grandstand and clubhouse were empty and quiet when World War II travel restrictions closed the track. *Courtesy of the Saratoga Room, Saratoga Springs Public Library.*

But Dewey didn't waver. Although Mallery kept pushing, trying to convince Dewey that Saratoga Race Course should reopen, the Saratoga Association's races were conducted for three years at Belmont Park. Grass and weeds grew on the track where legends were made and superstars often defeated.

World War II ended in 1945, and there was an unsuccessful push to hold a Saratoga meet that summer. Saratoga was back in business in 1946. The season began on Monday, August 5, and the *Saratogian* carried a bold banner headline on its front page that day: "Crowds Jam City for Return of Racing."[88] Yes, the old track was packed with a record opening-day crowd of 15,168.

Record-Setting Checkmate

Checkmate, a gelded son of British import Glen Athol out of the Vandal mare Full Cry, was the ultimate Saratoga horse and probably deserves a stake named in his honor. He compiled a record nineteen victories in four seasons, often competing against the top horses in training.

An 1875 foal, he was slow to develop, losing his only three starts at three and finally breaking his maiden in his sixth career start at St. Louis on June 19, 1879. He had moderate success in the Midwest, but when he came to Saratoga, he found a course he loved and won nine of eleven purse races.

In his first start at the Spa, on June 10, 1879, he faced Monitor for the first time. A future handicap champion in 1880, Monitor had lost his first four races in 1879, but his first start was a second in the Belmont Stakes to Spendthrift, that year's co-champion three-year-old male. Another of Monitor's early losses was a second to that year's champion older male, Bramble, so he clearly was competitive with top runners. Checkmate beat Monitor and ten other horses in that initial win at Saratoga. One day later, he finished second to Mintzner, who would later finish second in a handicap race to Bramble.

After two more purse wins, Checkmate finished in a dead heat with Lady Middleton in a six-furlong allowance race on August 1. In those days, if the two owners agreed, a dead heat was settled in a runoff. Lady Middleton and Checkmate met again after that day's card had ended, with the filly winning in a time that was a quarter of a second off the world record for the six-furlong distance.

Checkmate finished his initial Saratoga meet with six straight wins, including a walkover, and another race that involved only one other opponent, with no betting allowed.

At the age of five, in 1880, Checkmate became a multi-stakes winner. After beginning the season with a second in the National Handicap Sweepstakes at Washington, D.C., he won the Brighton Cup and the Willard Hotel Cup at that same track. Finishing second in the Brighton Cup was Monitor, and finishing second in the Willard Hotel was another Glen Athol gelding named Glenmore, who would face Checkmate several times in the future.

After winning the Rancocas Handicap at Pimlico for his third straight stakes win, Checkmate ran into an equine buzz saw named Luke Blackburn. One of the greatest horses to run in the nineteenth century, Luke Blackburn beat Checkmate in two purse events at Jerome Park and in his seasonal debut at Saratoga. Checkmate raced three more times at Saratoga in 1880, winning two purse events and losing by a length to three-year-old Elias Lawrence while conceding him twenty-one pounds.

The 1881 season was Checkmate's best at Saratoga and would serve as his swan song as a dominant handicap horse at the track. Following a lackluster beginning of the campaign in which he only won one purse event in eight starts, he returned to Saratoga and turned his entire season around.

Checkmate's first race at Saratoga, the Excelsior Sweepstakes, had the toughest field of his career. The favorite was the three-year-old gelding Crickmore, the previous year's co-champion two-year-old male with the great Hindoo. Crickmore had begun his sophomore season with a win in the Home-Bred Stakes at Pimlico and the Withers at Jerome Park and then lost to Hindoo by what the chart called a "scant length" in the Tidal and by three lengths in the Lorillard. After the Excelsior, Crickmore lost again to Hindoo in the United States Hotel and Kenner at Saratoga. However, Crickmore ended Hindoo's eighteen-race win streak in a period of four and a half months in September and beat him a week later in the Brighton Beach Purse at Sheepshead Bay.

The second favorite in the Excelsior was the Dwyer brothers' Ripple, another three-year-old who had beaten Checkmate on July 3 and July 4 at Monmouth Park in the Long Branch and Shrewsbury Handicaps. Third choice was that season's three-year-old filly champion, Thora, and fourth choice was the eight-year-old gelding Parole, a future Hall of Fame inductee who, despite advancing age and high imposts, had still managed to win that year's Westchester Cup and several purse events. Bruno, Oden and Umberto composed the rest of the field. At the beginning of the race, Thora,

Crickmore, Oden and Umberto assumed the early lead, with Checkmate and Parole in the rear. Turning for home, Thora took over what seemed to be an insurmountable lead, but Checkmate caught her at the seven-eighths pole—what we now call the eighth pole—and won by seven lengths in what the *New York Times* called "the greatest running of his life."[89] Although that newspaper was not shy about using hyperbole when reporting on turf events, in this particular case it might have been correct.

Not content to rest on his laurels, on July 21, Checkmate won the prestigious 2¼-mile Saratoga Cup. The favorite in the race was Checkmate's familiar rival Monitor, who had followed his championship 1880 season by winning the 2½-mile Baltimore Cup, finishing second in the Long Island Cup to Glenmore and winning the Monmouth Cup over Parole and Checkmate. However, the bettors had not factored in Checkmate's affinity for Saratoga, and at the finish, Checkmate prevailed by five lengths over Monitor, with Irish King and George McCulloch a badly beaten third and fourth, respectively.

Checkmate continued his successes at Saratoga by winning the 1½-mile Summer Handicap, with Thora finishing third; the Grand Prize of Saratoga; and three purse events. In the Grand Prize of Saratoga, he set a new stakes record by one and a half seconds despite carrying the high weight of 124 pounds, 12 pounds more than the next highest weight and 28 pounds more than the second-place finisher, Bushwacker.

His seven-race winning streak at Saratoga ended on August 18 in his last race that season at the Union Avenue track when he finished second to Bushwacker by two lengths in the two-mile Morrissey Stakes, while carrying 129 pounds to his opponent's minuscule 97. The *New York Times* resorted to its customary enthusiasm by describing the Morrissey as "one of the finest races ever witnessed" while stressing that "'Old Check's' defeat was due to the extra weight he carried."[90]

Checkmate exited Saratoga with a superlative record of seven wins in eight attempts from July 16 through August 18, and only a thirty-two-pound weight concession prevented him from a perfect season. He ended his post-Saratoga season with five wins from eight starts, including a victory in the three-mile Yorktown Centennial Handicap at Washington, D.C., and a badly beaten second to Thora in the Pimlico Stakes, with Monitor checking in a distant third. Checkmate's 1881 record of twelve wins, seven seconds and one third from twenty-four starts was enough for Thoroughbred Heritage to name him co-champion older horse with Glenmore.

Checkmate began his nine-year-old season in 1882 in promising fashion, defeating Hindoo in the Dixiana at Churchill Downs and finishing second to him in his next two races. However, after winning three of four races at St. Louis and Chicago, by the time he arrived in Saratoga, his age and high weights had finally caught up to him. His first race at the Spa was a sixth in the Cash Handicap as the favorite and high weight against only moderate competition, and that was followed by a win in a purse event, which was to be his last career win at Saratoga.

After a lackluster foray into Monmouth Park, where he won one of four starts, he returned to Saratoga and finished fifth of six horses in an allowance race and last of five in the Baden-Baden Handicap. In the latter, he was the last choice in the betting, and he justified the crowd's low opinion of his chances. Finishing ahead of him were familiar foes Bushwacker and Thora at third and fourth, respectively. The Baden-Baden was his last career race at Saratoga.

Checkmate's 1882 season did not improve after he left Saratoga, and in 1883, although he managed to win his second Dixiana, it was his only win in four starts at Churchill Downs. By August 1883, he had descended to running in selling races, continuing that trend in 1884, and his career ended in 1885 with a fourth and an ignominious twelfth and last in two selling races at Brighton Beach.

Checkmate's career record at Saratoga was nineteen wins and five seconds from twenty-seven starts, with his only off-the-board finishes occurring in his last season upstate.

Appendix

Hall of Fame and Other Champion Horses that Broke Their Maidens at Saratoga

HORSE	DATE	RACE	ODDS
Ruthless	July 28, 1866	2-y-o purse	unk
Katie Pease	August 22, 1872	Free handicap	unk
Regardless	July 21, 1873	Flash Stakes	unk
Olitipa	July 25, 1874	Flash Stakes	unk
Aristides	August 18, 1874	2-y-o handicap	unk
Sultana	August 14, 1875	2-y-o sweepstakes	unk
Vigil	August 1, 1876	maidens all ages	unk
Susquehanna	August 8, 1876	Kentucky Stakes	unk
Duke of Magenta	July 25, 1877	Flash Stakes	unk
Ferida	July 29, 1878	2-y-o maidens	unk
Belinda; Monitor 2nd	August 6, 1878	2-y-o allowance	unk
Glidelia	August 16, 1879	Day Boat Line Stakes	unk
Thora	July 23, 1880	2-y-o maidens	unk
Crickmore	July 27, 1880	Saratoga Stakes	unk
Eole	July 29, 1881	Allow. all ages	6-1
Hiawassa	July 30, 1881	Allow. all ages	unk

Horse	Date	Race	Odds
Firenze	August 2, 1886	2-y-o maidens	5-3
Connemara	August 5, 1886	2-y-o maidens	3-1
Delhi	August 15, 1903	Hopeful Stakes	4-1
Maskette	August 3, 1908	2-y-o allow.	1-4
Regret	August 8, 1914	Saratoga Special	1.60-1 (entry)
Dominant	August 2, 1915	United States Hotel	9-5
Puss in Boots; Dominant 2nd (2-1)	August 21, 1915	Grand Union Hotel	5-1
Omar Khayyam	August 4, 1916	2-y-o msw (f)	3-2
Cudgel	August 22, 1916	2-y-o msw	6-1
Milkmaid	August 26, 1918	2-y-o msw (f)	5-1
Vexatious; Milkmaid 2nd (11-20)	August 7, 1919	Alabama Stakes	7-2
Cleopatra	August 7, 1919	2-y-o msw (f)	7-2
Constancy; Cleopatra 9th (3-1)	August 16, 1919	Spinaway Stakes	9-1
Whiskaway	August 9, 1921	2-y-o allowance	5-1
Zev	August 5, 1922	2-y-o msw	7-5
Untidy	August 18, 1922	2-y-o msw	5-1
St. James	August 4, 1923	United States Hotel	13-5
American Flag	August 6, 1924	2-y-o msw	12-5
Black Maria	August 25, 1925	2-y-o allowance	18-5
Scapa Flow	July 31, 1926	United States Hotel	1-1
Reigh Count	August 29, 1927	2-y-o msw	9-5
High Strung	August 11, 1928	2-y-o msw	4-4
Gallant Fox	July 29, 1929	Flash Stakes	10-1
Burgoo King	August 18, 1931	2-y-o msw	2-1
Balladier	August 1, 1934	2-y-o allowance	5-2
High Fleet	July 30, 1935	2-y-o msw (f)	11-5
Lady Maryland	July 30, 1936	2-y-o msw (f)	15-1

HORSE	DATE	RACE	ODDS
Mar-Kell	August 6, 1941	2-y-o msw (f)	4.25-1
Devil Diver	August 8, 1941	2-y-o msw	3-2
Tea-Maker	August 11, 1948	3-y-o+up msw	50.65-1
Tom Fool	August 13, 1951	2-y-o msw	2-1
Career Boy	August 1, 1955	2-y-o msw	1.60-1
Nadir	August 15, 1957	2-y-o msw	2.60-1
Sword Dancer	August 23, 1958	2-y-o msw	1.15-1
Lamb Chop	August 21, 1962	2-y-o msw (f)	1-1
Moccasin	August 6, 1965	2-y-o msw (f)	7.90-1
Dark Mirage	August 2, 1967	2-y-o msw (f)	5.20-1
Ta Wee; Shuvee 5th (4-5)	August 13, 1968	2-y-o msw (f)	4.20-1
Shuvee	August 20, 1968	2-y-o msw (f)	3.70-1
Silent Screen	August 8, 1969	2-y-o msw	3.10-1
Café Prince	August 14, 1973	Op. cl., hurdles	1.50-1
Protagonist	August 24, 1973	2-y-o msw	5.70-1
Late Bloomer	August 23, 1977	3-y-o+up msw (f)	5.70-1
Plugged Nickle	August 4, 1979	2-y-o msw	8.80-1
Devil's Bag	August 20, 1983	2-y-o msw	1.10-1
Winning Colors; Epitome 2nd (6.20-1 entry)	August 13, 1987	2-y-o msw (f)	1.90-1
Easy Goer	August 19, 1988	2-y-o msw	3-5
Warm Spell	July 21, 1991	3-yo+up (hurdles)	exhibition
Flanders	August 10, 1994	2-y-o msw (f)	3-5
Beautiful Pleasure	August 25, 1997	2-y-o msw (f)	1.10-1
Lemon Drop Kid	August 1, 1998	2-y-o msw	1-1
Surfside	August 4, 1999	2-y-o msw (f)	.95-1
Macho Uno	July 26, 2000	2-y-o msw	3-4
Orientate	July 28, 2001	3-y-o+up msw	2-5
Miesque's Approval	August 13, 2001	2-y-o msw (turf)	9-10

APPENDIX

Horse	Date	Race	Odds
Storm Flag Flying	August 8, 2002	2-y-o msw (f)	3.65-1
English Channel	August 6, 2004	2-y-o msw (turf)	3.10-1
War Pass	July 28, 2007	2-y-o msw	6.90-1
Indian Blessing	August 30, 2007	2-y-o msw (f)	.85-1
Big Brown	September 3, 2007	2-y-o msw (turf)	14.70-1
Uncle Mo	August 25, 2010	2-y-o msw	9-10
My Miss Aurelia	July 22, 2011	2-y-o msw (f)	3.20-1

Notes

First Things First

1. *Saratogian*, "First Girl to Ride at Spa 'Has Real Ability,'" August 4, 1970, 4B.
2. *New York Times*, "Return Is $27.40," August 15, 1971, S1.
3. *New York Times*, "Debut of Sunday Cards at Spa Expected to Create Much Ado," July 27, 1975, S9.

Whichone

4. Bryan Field, "Whichone Captures the Saratoga Special," *New York Times*, August 11, 1929, S1.
5. J.P. Snodgrass, "Gallant Fox Picked to Beat Whichone Today in the Travers," *New York Evening Post*, August 16, 1930, 11.

A Pair of Dead-Heat Travers

6. Walter Vosburgh, *Racing in America: 1866–1921* (New York: The Jockey Club, 1922), 99–100.
7. *New York Times*, "The Turf: First Day at Saratoga," July 24, 1874, 1.
8. *New York Times*, "Saratoga, the Racing Season," July 26, 1874, 5.
9. *Spirit of the Times*, "The Summer Races," 1874, 613.
10. *New York Clipper*, "The Turf," August 1, 1874, 139.
11. *New York Daily Tribune*, "The Saratoga Meeting," July 27, 1874, 10.
12. Vosburgh, *Racing in America*, 100.
13. *Daily Racing Form*, "Saratoga: Travers Ends in Alpha-Golden Ticket Dead Heat," August 27, 2012.

TRAVERS TRAINER MARY HIRSCH STANDS ALONE

14. *New York Times*, "Miss Hirsch Ask Jockey Club for a License to Train Horses," February 8, 1933, 24.
15. Ibid.
16. *New York Times*, "License to Miss Hirsch Upsets Racing Precedent," July 29, 1934, S8.
17. *New York Times*, "Miss Hirsch Licensed as Trainer by Stewards of the Jockey Club," April 3, 1935, 27.
18. *New York Times*, "Captain Argo Wins Feature at Miami," March 28, 1935, 28.
19. *New York Post*," No Sir Kind to Mary Hirsch and Her Coffee-Loving Pals," August 28, 1936, 20.
20. *New York Times*, "Parker Corning, Ex-Lawmaker, Dies," May 25, 1943, 23.
21. *Schenectady Gazette*, "'Queen Mary' Rules Over 'Sport of Kings' at Spa," August 17, 1937, 4.
22. *New York Times*, "Wed in Racing Romance," April 1, 1940, 3.

NINETEENTH-CENTURY STEEPLECHASING AND HURDLES RACING

23. *American Turf Register* 29 (1858): 34.
24. *New York Herald*, August 7, 1864, 5.
25. *Daily Saratogian*, August 8, 1864, 1.
26. Ibid.
27. *American Turf Register* 29 (1858): 34.
28. Peter Winants, *Steeplechasing: A Complete History of the Sport in North America* (Lanham: Derrydale Press, 2000), 24.
29. *American Turf Register* (1870): 24.
30. Winants, *Steeplechasing*, 21.
31. *Spirit of the Times*, "The Second Day of Racing," August 20, 1870, 3.
32. *New York Times*, "Saratoga Races," July 18, 1871, 4.
33. Ibid.

COMMON ERRORS ABOUT SARATOGA RACING

34. *New York Times*, "Saratoga Still Entertaining Very Large Crowds of Summer Visitors," August 24, 1902, 27.
35. *New York Times*, "Many Upsets in Golf Play," July 25, 1919, 13.
36. *Troy Times Record*, "Clare Court, Has Charm, Tradition Typical of Spa," July 31, 1948, 5.
37. *Saratogian*, "Saratoga Still Most Beautiful Racetrack," July 22, 1940.
38. *Saratogian*, "Over Half Million in Purses for Thirty Day Race Meeting Here," July 28, 1928, 12.

Hopeful and Spinaway Winner Tanya

39. *New York Times*, "Hermis, First Romping, Surprised Horsemen," May 22, 1904, 13.
40. *New York Times*, "Tanya's Spinaway Stake," August 4, 1904, 3.
41. *New York Times*, "Tanya Won Big Stakes," August 14, 1904, 6.
42. *New York Sunday Telegraph*, "Hopeful Stakes Easy for Tanya," August 14, 1904, 2.

Surprising Winners

43. Debra Ginsburg, "Jim Dandy," *Backstretch* (July/August 2000): 158.

An Ode to the Popular Molly Brant

44. Vosburgh, *Racing in America*, 195.
45. *New York Times*, "Hurricana's Great Day," August 17, 1904, 5.
46. *New York Times*, "Dolly Spanker Wins from Molly Brant," August 25, 1905, 4.

The Notorious Gottfried Walbaum

47. *New York Times*, "The Prize Fight Between Dunn and Davis; Dunn the Victor," May 18, 1865.
48. Gottfried Walbaum, *Reminiscences of Gottfried Walbaum* (N.p.: self-published, 1931), 5.
49. Ibid, 8.
50. *New York Times*, December 28, 1891.
51. Walbaum, *Reminiscences*, 1.
52. Paul Roberts and Isabelle Taylor, *The Spa, Saratoga's Legendary Race Course* (London: Turnberry Consulting Limited, 2011), 48.
53. Hugh Bradley, *Such Was Saratoga* (New York: Doubleday, Doran and Company Inc., 1940), 237–38.
54. *New York Evening Post*, December 8, 1936, 30.
55. Walbaum, *Reminiscences*, "Saratoga," 13.
56. Ibid.
57. *New York Sun*, "Gamblers' Jewels in Auction To-Day," May 16, 1918, 16.

East versus West in the 1879 Travers

58. *Daily Racing Form*, "In Early Days at Saratoga," August 6, 1921, 1.
59. *New York Times*, "The Races at Saratoga: An Unlucky Day for the Favorites," July 20, 1879, 7.
60. *New York Daily Tribune*, "Defeat of Spendthrift and Bramble," July 21, 1879, 8.
61. Ibid.
62. *New York Daily Tribune*, "Defeat of Spendthrift and Bramble."
63. *Daily Racing Form*, "Falsetto's Only Failure," March 19, 1916, 1.

THINGS TO KNOW ABOUT SARATOGA

64. *New York Times*, "Fast Fillies to Meet Nedna, Victor in the Alabama, Again," August 15, 1922.
65. Landon Manning, "The NYRA and Saratoga," *Saratogian*, July 31, 1961, 1, 4.

THREE EQUINE METEORS

66. *Daily Racing Form*, "Novelty Wins the Futurity for S.C. Hildreth," September 1, 1910, 1.
67. *Daily Racing Form*, "Mr. Keene's Estimate of Novelty," September 3, 1916, 1.
68. Vosburgh, *Racing in America*, 205; *Daily Racing Form*, "Novelty's Son Wins Brazilian Prize," November 20, 1919, 1.
69. John Hervey, "Two Bostonians," *American Race Horses, 1936* (New York: Sagamore Press, 1936), 34.
70. Ibid.

GATES CLOSED ON UNION AVENUE

71. Nellie Bly, "Our Wickedest Summer Resort," *New York World*, 21.
72. *New York Times*, "Saratoga," September 11, 1892, 10.
73. Bradley, *Such Was Saratoga*, 182.
74. Ibid, 205.
75. Edward Hotaling, *They're Off: Racing at Saratoga* (Syracuse, NY: Syracuse University Press, 1995), 136.
76. *New York Times*, "Saratoga's Gamblers in Peril," August 4, 1886.
77. *New York Times*, "Saratoga's Lovely Weather," August 19, 1890, 4.
78. [New York] *Evening Telegram*, "Saratoga Gamblers Pulled," August 29, 1889, 1.
79. Walbaum, *Reminiscences*, "Saratoga," 1.
80. *New York Times*, "To Extend Its Meeting," January 15, 1894, 8.
81. *New York Times*, "The Saratoga Failure," August 7, 1895, 6.
82. *New York Times*, "The Week at Saratoga Springs," August 11, 1895, 13.
83. *New York Times*, "Saratoga Race Track Sold," November 2, 1900.
84. *New York Times*, "New York Racing Ends August 31," August 6, 1910, 5.
85. *New York Times*, "Betting Upheld by Court Decision," October 14, 1912.
86. *Saratogian*, "Race-Lovers by Thousands Will Open the Meeting," August 1, 1913, 1.
87. *New York Times*, "Cock O' the Walk Wins the Saratoga," August 3, 1913, 52.
88. *Saratogian*, "Crowds Jam City for Return of Racing," August 5, 1946, 1.

RECORD-SETTING CHECKMATE

89. *New York Times*, "The Racing at Saratoga," July 17, 1881, 2.
90. *New York Times*, "Grand Race at Saratoga," August 19, 1881, 5.

Index

About the Authors

A llan Carter was a law librarian at the New York State Library for thirty years, retiring in 2003. In 1995, he was given the West Excellence in Government Law Librarianship Award. Prominent among his many publications were *New York State Constitution: Sources of Legislative Intent* and *Public Library Law in New York State*. Immediately upon his retirement, he joined the National Museum of Racing as an assistant to the historian and became the museum's historian in 2004.

M ike Kane was a newspaper sportswriter and columnist for thirty years, twenty-five of them at the *Schenectady Gazette*. In 2005, he began a nearly five-year tour as the communications officer at the National Museum of Racing. He won the Red Smith Kentucky Derby Writing Contest five consecutive years and is a former president of the National Turf Writers and Broadcasters Association. An active freelance writer and photographer, he is the author of *Minor in Name Only: The History of the Adirondack Red Wings*.